Roots of Passion
Essays on Cynthia Ozick

Edited by Jane Statlander-Slote, PhD.

Llumina
PRESS

© 2016 Jane Statlander-Slote, PhD.

All rights reserved. No part of this publication may be reproduced or transmitted in any form or by any means electronic or mechanical, including photocopy, recording, or any information storage and retrieval system, without permission in writing from both the copyright owner and the publisher.

No patent liability is assumed with respect to the use of the information contained herein. Although every precaution has been taken in the preparation of this book, the publisher and author assume no responsibility for errors or omissions. Neither is any liability assumed for damages resulting from the use of the information contained herein.

Requests for permission to make copies of any part of this work should be mailed to Permissions Department, Llumina Press, 7580 NW 5th Street #16535, Fort Lauderdale, FL 33318.

ISBN: 978-1-62550-295-7 (PB)
978-1-62550-297-1 (HC)
978-1-62550-269-4 (EB)

Printed in the United States of America by Llumina Press

Library of Congress Control Number: 2016904492

Contents

Preface Dan Walden: A Tribute *by Cynthia Ozick* — i

Introduction *by Jane Statlander-Slote* — iii

1. **"Envy"** Cynthia Ozick Meets Melanie Klein *by Andrew Gordon* — 1

2. **A Portrait of the Vilde Chaye as a Jewish Artist** *by Joseph Lowin* — 8

3. **With James and Ozick in Paris: The Ambassadors and Foreign Bodies** *by Sanford Marovitz* — 17

4. **Cythia Ozick and the Christian Reader** *by Victor Strandberg* — 37

5. **Cynthia Ozick's Classical Feminism** *by Daniel Walden* — 62

6. **Waiting for Moshiach: Reading Absence in Ozick's The Messiah of Stockholm** *by Jessica Lang* — 72

7. **Interview with Cynthia Ozick** *by Jane Statlander-Slote and Alessandra Farkas* — 86

8. **Cynthia Ozick: A Jewish Woman Writer And Her Many Paradoxes** *by Daniela Fargione* — 96

Preface

Dan Walden: A Tribute

By Cynthia Ozick

When Irving Howe notoriously wrote off the future of American Jewish fiction as destined to come to a halt with the end of the immigrant narrative, there was much he did not foresee. Perhaps he could not: he was wedded to the landscape and mind-set of *The World of Our Fathers*, his masterly evocation of the turn-of-the-twentieth-century flood of Yiddish-speaking Eastern European Jews, those humble begetters of the literary offspring whose illustrious names we know. He did not foresee the young writers who came into prominence as much as four generations beyond the immigrant era; he did not foresee the young Soviet emigrants, with their speedily absorbed and gifted English and their radically different perspectives and honed ironies. But who – even so astutely insightful a social and literary critic as Howe – can be faulted for misconstruing the future of a culture?

It may be, though, that Howe can fairly be charged with missing, or at least overlooking, a significant signpost present in his own generation: the remarkable journal founded, edited, cultivated, and broadened by Dan Walden. For all the decades since it came into being, *Studies in American Jewish Literature* has been an antenna, a pulse-taker, a harbinger. *SAJL* held out an analytic embrace for every tendency, every subject and style. Its discerning editor neither saw nor identified nor declared a stopping-point for the burgeoning of themes and perspectives. Dan Walden understood that the Jewish literary enterprise is as horizonless as it is inevitable (or call it endemic): how else account for Babel and Kafka, Stephen Zweig and H.G. Adler, André Schwarz-Bart and Irène Némirovsky, Giorgio Bassani and Natalia Ginzburg, Howard Jacobson and the two Roths, Henry and Philip? In the making of a lasting literature, language and history, and the power of the local and the idiosyncratically particular, are ineluctably entwined.

Hence the *American* in this distinguished journal's title: the American voice in the American idiom, American societal complexity played out on Whitmanian American soil. It was Dan Walden's uncommon social and historical penetration that made him a pioneer in black literary studies well before the newer term "African American" came into general use, and long before the inauguration of *SAJL*. What he was pursuing, even then, was the richness and distinctiveness of the particular.

It was a British Jewish writer, Israel Zangwill, who in a popular drama applauded by President Theodore Roosevelt lauded the concept of the "melting pot." Its theme was of an amalgamation so thorough that the original elements would be effectively dissolved. But the melting pot is the opposite of pluralism, which takes on a different metaphor, that of a weaving or braiding, each strand explicit in its texture and hue even as it contributes to the composition of the perfected fabric. Multiculturism, a more recent literary and social thesis, in its unharmonious fostering of group rivalry grounded in competitive victimhood, differs even more radically from traditional American pluralism. Dan Walden's aim in *SAJL* was consciously otherwise: it was to honor the individuality of the strand while prizing its integral presence – a purposefulness that renders irrelevant Philip Roth's insistence that his American heritage must necessarily overcome his Jewish patrimony.

Dan Walden's overriding contribution – the cornucopia of encouragement that was his credo as teacher, scholar, and editor – is precisely here: a passionate recognition that there is bottomless interest, vivacity, complexity, illumination, and above all astonishment, in every new turn in American Jewish (or, as it is nowadays more frequently named, Jewish American) writing. If he has, from the very start, been prescient, it is because of a generosity so open, so welcoming, so limitless, and so profoundly characteristic, that, like some tirelessly pulsing magnet, it has gathered in unpredictable marvels. He knew no stopping-point. He defined no horizon. He was, and remains, a champion of literary possibility.

Introduction

Jane Statlander-Slote

The appearance of this volume is an important step in revitalizing the critical study of Cynthia Ozick's literary output, and in renewing interest in this dazzlingly talented writer. Most of what was published about her work was written from the mid-60s to the 80s--- with the greatest number of essays appearing during the 1970s. However, for the most part--- except for two studies in the early 90s--- Ozick readers, it seemed, fell silent; or worse, forgot how good a writer she was and is. Nevertheless, one person kept the torch burning: The late Daniel Walden, who asked me in 2001 to write a volume on Cynthia Ozick for his Jewish Writers Series, which appeared the following year; and, again, this present collection, planned to have been co-edited by me and Dan, was conceived by Dan in respect and admiration for his good friend. That admiration and appreciation has now come full circle: with Dan's demise, it is Cynthia Ozick who now pays tribute. This volume, then, is the first full scale collection of critical reactions to Cynthia Ozick's work in a decade and a half, and, as well, is a deep expression of Daniel Walden and Cynthia Ozick's mutual appreciation.

Unlike Philip Roth, the secular, post-modernist, Newark, Bad Boy, Ozick's work is ablaze with moral imperatives that pit the Judaic world against the Gentile one; that is to say, it sets monotheism in conflict with polytheism and Hellenism with Judaism. Her writing, paradoxically, goes even further in elevating rationality over imagination; and, in Jewish cultural terms, draws out the conflict of mind sets between a rational, skeptical *Litvac* (Lithuanian) tradition and a mystical, emotion-driven *Galizian* one. The term, *mitnagged*, from the Hebrew word, "against" is what one of *Litvac* origins uses to be distinguished from the irrational, too imaginative, despised other, the Galizian. In all of this, however, is died in 2013. Chapter One by Jane Statlander-Slote is a panoramic, sweeping look at Ozick and her work. In Chapter Two, Joseph Lowin creates an expansive bu;t thorough overview of Ozick, her career, and personal life. Chapter Three by Andrew Gordon entitled "'Envy': Cynthia Ozick Meets Melanie Klein" is a keen psychological investigation of Kleinian concepts at work in Ozick's writing. In Chapter Four Victor Strandberg in "'Identity' in the Personal Correspondence of Victor Strandberg and Cynthia Ozick" traces the theme of *identity* as Ozick perceives and reveals it in their decades-long letter-writing correspondence. Sandford Marovitz, in Chapter Five, examines identity and the clash of the Jewish and Gentile worlds in "'Messiah of Stockholm' and 'Foreign Bodies'". Chapter Six, is Daniel Walden's "Cynthia Ozick's Classical Feminism" exploring Ozick's female identity through her life and work. Chapter Seven, Jessica Lang's "'Waiting for Moshiach: Reading Absence in Ozick's *The Messiah of Stockholm*, examines the influence of Bruno Schultz's work on Ozick writings and, as with David Grossman and Philip Roth , served as a creative guide. Chapter Eight is an interview with Cynthia Ozick conducted by Jane Statlander-Slote and Alessandra Farkas. Chapter Nine, an essay on Ozick as a Jewish writer, by Daniela Fargione, explores the sticky issue of describing Ozick not just as a female writer; but a Jewish one as well.

Roots of Passion
Essays on Cynthia Ozick

1. "Envy"

Cynthia Ozick Meets Melanie Klein

Andrew Gordon

Cynthia Ozick's story "Envy; or, Yiddish in America" shows the corrosive effects of envy on the life of the lonely, aging Yiddish poet Edelshtein. Edelshtein is consumed with envy of Ostrover, a famous Yiddish novelist known from English translations of his stories. He feels that Ostrover has both cuckolded him and bested him in literary success. Edelshtein believes he could become as famous as Ostrover if he too had a translator into English. Without the translator, he fears his poems will die along with him and the dying Yiddish language. The story seems to illustrate the psychological insights of Melanie Klein about the unconscious mechanisms behind envy: "I consider that envy is an oral-sadistic and anal-sadistic expression of destructive impulses, operative from the beginning of life…" (Klein, ix). So long as Edelshtein operates out of envy, he will remain caught in a vicious cycle, in an infantile, self-destructive state, thwarted in his attempts to love or to be creative. He will continue to feel persecuted by Ostrover, which is really a form of internal persecution. As Klein writes, "When this occurs, the good object is felt to be lost, and with it inner security" (84).

"Envy," which is included in Ozick's 1969 collection, *The Pagan Rabbi*, is reminiscent of Bellow's *Herzog* (1965). Both are profound psychological anatomies, detailed dissections of a single suffering character, a victim who is nevertheless in many ways his own worst enemy. Both stories are delicately poised between the comic and the tragic. Both protagonists are intellectuals who rail against the "Wasteland outlook" and defend Jewish humanism. Herzog rejects "the commonplaces of the Wasteland outlook, the cheap mental stimulants of Alienation, the cant and rant of pipsqeaks about Inauthenticity and Forlornness" (Bellow 75). And Edelshtein writes, "*Mamaloshen* doesn't produce *Wastelands*. No alienation, no nihilism, no dadism" (Ozick163). But aside from their insights and eloquence, both men are also cuckolds and *shlimazels*, obsessed and half-crazy, consumed with jealousy or envy and the desire for revenge, and both compose many mental letters they never send. What Gersbach is for Herzog, Ostrover is for Edelshtein. The difference is that Herzog is twenty years younger than Edelshtein, has family and friends and more inner resources, and thus is more capable of love and of recovery. *Herzog* ends with the hero at peace, in the summertime in the country, putting his house in order, and awaiting the visit of a woman who loves him. "Envy" ends with the hero in the winter in New York City, alone and embittered, raging on the phone at an anti-Semite. Herzog matures a bit in the course of the narrative, but Edelshtein, despite being much older than Herzog, is prevented from growing up by the force of his all-consuming envy.

Edelshtein is in many ways sympathetic, a little guy struggling to survive, lost in America. Although, as the opening sentence says, Edelshtein has been "an American for forty years," he is not really American but feels like a displaced person (129). He talks with an accent, and he cannot write poetry in English. There is no old country to which he can return, for the European Jewish culture and the Yiddish language has been practically eradicated by the Holocaust. Even Israel is hostile to Yiddish: "Yiddish was inhabited by the past, the new Jews did not want it" (135). So the only hope, as the title suggests, is "Yiddish in America." Yet, ironically, in America, Yiddish is a lost cause. Edelshtein makes a meager living lecturing on the subject to bored audiences of elderly Jews. "To speak of Yiddish was to preside over a funeral. He was a rabbi who had survived his whole congregation" (131). The story is filled with images of death, of a murdered people and a murdered language, and of Yiddish speakers as the living dead, corpses, or ghosts.

To make matters worse, Edelshtein is 67, facing mortality and pondering the meaning of his life and his legacy. Because he is a widower with no children, his only heirs are his poems, which no one reads anymore because so few read Yiddish. So he searches for someone to translate them into English, but in vain. Judging from the samples of his work in the story, Edelshtein had talent in his youth, but he is a minor poet writing in a minor language, poetry loses more than fiction in translation, and there is little money in it for translators or publishers.

So one cannot help but feel sorry for this old man who mourns the death of Yiddish, which has contributed to his sense of isolation and failure. Nevertheless, Edelshtein is also, as mentioned, a comic fool, a *shlimazel*, and his own worst enemy. He defends Yiddish and the Jews who perished in the Holocaust, but even as he does so, "he knew he lied, lied, lied. . . . He felt himself an obscenity. What did the dead of Jews have to do with his own troubles? His cry was ego and more ego. His own stew, foul. Whoever mourns the dead mourns himself " (157).

As Melanie Klein says, "envy is an oral-sadistic and anal-sadistic expression of destructive impulses." Thus the "foul stew" of Edelshtein's ego. The story is filled with anal imagery; it is, as Victor Strandberg says, "a catalogue of decay" (Strandberg 89).

There are references to "mud," to "urine and dirt" (Ozick 130), to "rubble and offal" (140), to "turds"(155), to "a sewer" (170), numerous mentions of snot, mucus, and vomit, and lots of spitting, burping, and belching. In one of his dreams, Edelshtein cries out, "Thou shalt see my asshole!"(132).

In Vorovsky, one of Ostrover's translators, Ozick creates a double for Edelshtein who expresses Edelshtein's envy and anal sadism. Both men blame their wasted lives on the hated Ostrover. "'I would like to make a good strong b.m. on your friend Ostrover,'"says Vorovsky (Ozick 148). Vorovsky spent 17 years writing a dictionary no one wants to buy and Edelshtein has spent his entire life writing Yiddish poems no one wants to read. Vorovsky says, "'Do you know what a bilingual German-English mathematical dictionary is good for? . . . . Toilet paper. . . . Do you know what poems are good for? The same'" (149). The living room of Vorovsky's apartment is lined with 75 cardboard boxes filled with unsold copies of the dictionary. Edelshtein thinks of Vorovsky, "It was his fate to swallow what he first excreted" (171). As Elaine M. Kauvar notes, "that situation mirrors Edelshtein's" (Kauvar 55).

In one scene, Edelshtein even wishes he could stop caring and completely let go, becoming a crazy drunk like Vorovsky, and he imagines Vorovsky telling him that first he needs to study failure some more. Like Edelshtein, Vorovsky is an old man driven so crazy by failure that he loses self-control and wallows in "his own stew, foul. " Vorovsky's anal and urethral sadism turn against himself. He suffers from bouts of hysterical laughter at the absurdity of his life, during which he loses all bodily control:

Vorovsky laughed and said 'Messiah' and sucked the pillow spitting. His face was a flood: tears ran upside down into his eyes, over his forehead, saliva sprang up in puddles around his ears. He was spitting, crying, burbling, he gasped, wept, spat. His eyes were bloodshot, the whites showed like slashes, wounds; he still wore his hat. He laughed, he was still laughing. His pants were wet, the fly open, now and then seeping (170).

With his crying, drooling, and incontinence, Vorovsky is an old man reverting to infancy, exaggerating tendencies also present in Edelshtein.

Edelshtein is not so much an infant as an overgrown boy, and his married friends the Baumzweigs his substitute parents. He hangs around their apartment and even spends the night sleeping in the room formerly occupied by their sons. Significantly, he connects Paula Baumzweig with his own mother. When Edelshtein recites one of his poems in their apartment, Paula "would always kiss Edelshtein on the forehead," like a proud mother rewarding a son (133). He notices "the tiny blue veins all over Paula's neck" (157), and soon after he remembers that "his mother's neck too was finely veined" (158).

According to Klein, envy originates in a disturbance of the primary object relation with the mother. Envy, she claims, is a kind of oral attack on the mother and the mother's breast. As young Hannah, Vorovsky's niece, accuses Vorovsky and Edelshtein, "'you envy, you eat people up with your disgusting old age–cannibals. . . .'" (175). She also calls them "parasites"(175) and "bloodsuckers"(172) and labels Edelshtein "Mr. Vampire" (173). Hannah's cruel accusations, although exaggerated, express truth about the unconscious origins of envy in infantile sadism.

Although Edelshtein's memory of his mother seems positive, all his relationships with women in the story are contentious. He quarreled with his late wife Mireleh, who was barren due to multiple miscarriages, "was vindictive about Edelshtein's sperm count," and was also unfaithful to Edelshtein with Ostrover (135). He has a falling out with his friend Paula Baumzweig. And although he tries to flatter Hannah into being his translator, when she refuses, he hits her in the mouth and curses her. Earlier he referred to a young boy he loved as being "nearer than my mother's mouth" (162), yet now he strikes a woman in the mouth. His hostility suggests an ambivalence toward women, perhaps rooted in an unstable relationship with his mother. It is then not surprising that he insults Paula as "'mother of puppydogs'" (151).

According to Klein, envy originates in an unconscious attack on the mother's breast, and Pesha, Ostrover's wife, Edelshtein deprecates as cowlike, "a cube with low-slung udders" (134). Later, when he spies on the Baumzweigs as they sleep, he notes that Paula's "breasts had dropped sidewise and, although still very fat, hung in pitiful creased bags of mole-dappled skin" (158). He says that she is like a "cow to the sight" (157). As Klein writes, envy aims "to put badness, primarily bad excrements and bad parts of the self, into the mother, and first of all into her breast, in order to spoil and destroy her. In the deepest sense this means destroying her creativeness" (Ozick 7). Thus the ugly, bovine breasts in the story qualify as what Klein calls "the bad breast."

Envy is among the seven deadly sins and, says Klein, "it is unconsciously felt to be the greatest sin of all, because it spoils and harms the good object which is the source of life. . . . The feeling of having injured and destroyed the primal object impairs the individual's trust in the sincerity of his later relationships and makes him doubt his capacity for love and goodness" (Klein 20). Thus envy is inevitably self-destructive. Edelshtein is filled with rage: against Nazis, against American Jews, and against the hand that life has dealt him. He spends a lot of the story in juvenile temper tantrums. He needs an object to hate, so he settles on Ostover. But his envy of Ostover is corrosive, eating him up, destroying his enjoyment of life and his creativity.

The Baumzweigs share his envy of Ostrover; in fact, it is the main bond of their friendship. Yet Paula Baumzweig correctly calls their trip to hear Ostrover speak at the Y "'self-mortification'" and "'self-flagellation'" (Ozick 141). Waiting in the auditorium for Ostrover to appear, "Edelshtein felt paralyzed." He thinks of a poem he could be writing and wishes he were home to write it; "the hall around him seemed preposterous, unnecessary, why was he here?" (142). As Melanie Klein writes, "envy of creativeness is a fundamental element in the disturbance of the creative process. . . The super-ego figure on which strong envy has been projected becomes particularly persecutory and interferes with thought processes and with every productive activity, ultimately with creativeness" (Klein 40). Edelshtein is there because his obsession with Ostrover is really a form of self-punishment. Ostrover is a projection of Edelshtein's persecutory super-ego, and the more he envies Ostrover, the more his hatred returns to persecute him.

The only hope for Edelshtein lies in clinging to the remnants of the good object, which is Yiddish, the *mamaloshen* (mother tongue) which in this story represents the good mother. Edelshtein writes to Hannah, "Fifty years ago my mother lived in Russia and spoke only broken Russian, but her Yiddish was like silk" (157). But as Yiddish fades, Edelshtein becomes increasingly desperate. He fantasizes that young Hannah will save him by translating his poetry and also save Yiddish for future generations. For Ostrover, Hannah is both a symbolic daughter, substitute for the child he never had, and a symbolic mother who will carry Yiddish in her womb and bear him into the future, reborn. "Grow old in Yiddish, Hannah, and carry fathers and uncles into the future with you," he writes (156). But Hannah, who hates the old and has no use for Yiddish, denounces Edelshtein and cruelly rejects him. In his fantasy, he turned Hannah into an idealized object, a recreation of the good mother, the *yiddishe mama*. But when he encounters the real Hannah, she turns instead into the spoiled, bad object, destroying his fantasy. Writes Klein, "The idealized object is much less integrated in the ego than the good object, since it stems predominantly from persecutory anxiety and much less from the capacity for love." (Klein 26) Idealized objects cannot be sustained, which lead to "instability in relationships" (27).

Thus the story ends with Edelshtein in despair, rejected by Hannah, yet ironically phoning a Christian evangelist for consolation, only to be subjected to a vicious anti-Semitic harangue. Why this self-punishing maneuver? As Klein writes of the envious person, "The need for punishment, which finds satisfaction by the increased devaluation of the self, leads to a vicious circle" (85).

Yet Edelshtein, as Joseph Lowin says, "lacks a tragic dimension" (Lowin 28).

Even at the end, railing on the phone against the anti-Semite, he is still the *shlimazel*, more pathetic clown than tragic figure. "In 'Envy,'" writes Sarah Blacher Cohen, "Ozick continually alternates from the dour to the droll" (Cohen 48). Jealousy can be the subject of a tragedy, as in *Othello*, but envy cannot. Envy "implies the subject's relation to one person only and goes back to the earliest exclusive relationship with the mother.

Jealousy is based on envy, but involves a relationship to at least two people" (Klein 6). Tragedy occurs in the realm of oedipal conflict, but the envious person never reaches that stage and thus never really grows up.

WORKS CITED

Bellow, Saul. Herzog. 1965; New York: Viking, 1976.

Cohen, Sarah Blacher. Cynthia Ozick's Comic Art: From Levity to Liturgy. Bloomington: Indiana University Press, 1994.

Kauvar, Elaine M. Cynthia Ozick's Fiction: Tradition and Invention. Bloomington: Indiana University Press, 1993.

Klein, Melanie. Envy and Gratitude: A Study of Unconscious Sources. NY: Basic Books, 1957.

Lowin, Joseph. Cynthia Ozick. Boston: Twayne, 1988.

Ozick, Cynthia. "Envy; or, Yiddish in America." Jewish American Stories. Ed. Irving Howe. New York: New American Library, 1977: 129-77.

Strandberg, Victor. Greek Mind/Jewish Soul: The Conflicted Art of Cynthia Ozick. Madison: University of Wisconsin Press, 1994.

2. A Portrait of the Vilde Chaye as a Jewish Artist

Joseph Lowin

In conversation, one hears a soft, youthful tinkle, clear as a bell. Then there is the unfailing Old World politeness, the refinement of language, and a bright eagerness in the voice to share her thoughts, to hold nothing back. Yet, if the voice is poetry, the words are prophecy. One will hear this in the deep insights, the well-wrought thought, the keen incisiveness, and the sharp wit. These will come later—but they will come.

There is simultaneously something very young and something decidedly hoary about the persona of Cynthia Ozick. She herself recognizes this duality. In "The Break," a virtuoso comic performance that first appeared in the Spring 1994 issue of *Antaeus,* her younger self (who goes by the Hebrew name of Shoshana) solemnly announces her disengagement from the "white-haired, dewlapped, thick-waisted, thick-lensed hag" (who goes by the Greek name of Cynthia)—a writer disgustingly devoid of that hunger for success that drives great artists. What does this "seventeen-to-twenty-two-year-old" energetic, ambitious writer, who sees a whole row of luminescent novels on the horizon, have in common with this sixty-six-year-old woman who is resigned to her failures? "I would not trade places with her," shouts Shoshana, "for all the china in Teaneck."

Cynthia Ozick was born in New York City on April 17, 1928, the second of two children. She subsequently moved to the Bronx with her parents, Celia (Regelson) and William Ozick, who were the proprietors of the Park View Pharmacy in the Pelham Bay section. Her parents had come to America from the severe northwest region of Russia.

More important for an insight into Ozick's temperament, they came from the Litvak [Lithuanian] Jewish tradition of that region. That is a tradition of skepticism, rationalism, and antimysticism, opposed to the exuberant emotionalism of the Hasidic community that flourished in the Galitzianer [Galician] portion of Eastern Europe. This explains, perhaps, why the Hasidic rebbe in Ozick's story "Bloodshed" is such a reasonable man, almost a Litvak. Ozick herself, she does not tire of repeating, is a *misnaged,* an opponent of mystic religion. In her stories, however, she wallows in mysticism.

Ozick describes the life of her parents with reverence. It was not unusual for them to put in a fourteen-hour day at the drugstore, often closing the store at one in the morning. Cynthia herself served as the delivery girl of prescriptions. Ozick describes her mother's life as a life of total generosity, of lavishness, of exuberance, of untrammeled laughter. Her father, a discreet, quiet man, a *talmid hokhem* [a Jewish scholar], who also knew both Latin and German from his Russian gymnasium years, ground and mixed powders and entered prescriptions meticulously in his record book. It is not without interest that, according to his daughter, he wrote beautiful Hebrew paragraphs and had a Talmudist's rationalism.

However, life was not without its childhood pain. At the age of five and a half, Ozick entered heder, the Yiddish-Hebrew "room" where, in the America of those years, Jewish pupils were sent for religious instruction. There she was confronted by a rabbi who told Cynthia's *bobe* [grandmother], who had accompanied her granddaughter to school, in Yiddish, "Take her home; a girl doesn't have to study." Ozick dates her feminism to that time and is especially grateful to her grandmother for bringing her back to school the very next day and insisting that she be accepted. Even the rabbi, to whom Ozick appears to bear no lasting animosity, had occasion to be grateful, for this girl had, as the rabbi would quickly learn, a *goldene kepele* [golden little head] that caught on quickly to the lessons. Ozick owes her knowledge of Yiddish to a certain Rabbi Meskin, a teacher who "taught girls as zealously as he taught boys," and to her grandmother.

At P.S. 71 in the Bronx, the hurt was of a different order. At home and in heder, the young girl was considered intelligent. In school, on the contrary, she was made to feel inadequate. She was, however, excellent in the bookish arts, such as grammar, spelling, reading, and writing. While Ozick describes the Pelham Bay section of the Bronx as a lovely place, she found it "brutally difficult to be a Jew" there. She remembers having stones thrown at her and being called a Christ-killer as she ran past the two churches in her neighborhood. She was particularly uncomfortable in school because she would not, on principle, sing the particularly Christian Christmas carols, and was made "a humiliated public example for that." While writing *The Cannibal Galaxy*, a novel set in a Jewish all-day school, she asserts, "I thought of my own suffering, deeply suffering wormlike childhood in grade school; and of my mother's endurances in grade school as an immigrant child.... Carelessness in a teacher of small children can burn in impotence for life, like a brand or horrible sign."

All was not dreariness in her childhood, however, for there remained the world of books. In "A Drugstore in Winter," Ozick describes how reading and "certain drugstore winter dusks" came together thanks to the traveling library that arrived in her neighborhood every other week. She recalls that the librarians would come into the Park View Pharmacy after their rounds to have a cup of hot coffee at the fountain. Ozick would come in behind them, having chosen the two fattest volumes from the boxes of books and magazines offered to her. With these books in her hands, she was transported to another world.

She began her reading with fairy tales. From her older brother, she received the perfect birthday present—books. These books had a magical effect, transforming her from a doltish schoolgirl into "who I am"—a reader, and perhaps a writer. "Some day when I am free of P.S. 71, I will write stories. Meanwhile, in winter dusk, in the Park View, in the secret bliss of the Violet Fairy Book, I both see and do not see how these grains of life will stay forever."

Ozick owes her metamorphosis into a writer to the fact that her mother's brother, Abraham Regelson, was a Hebrew poet of no mean reputation. She feels that, somehow, he paved the way for her to embark on such a "strange" career—writer. Because of him, she says, "it seemed quite natural to belong to the secular world of literature." At one time, she attributed her freedom to choose such a "frivolous" career as writer to her gender. "My father loved me," she told an interviewer, "but I think one of the reasons from earliest childhood I felt free to be a writer is that if I had been a boy, I would have had to go be something else."

School became a serious pursuit for Ozick when she entered HUNTER COLLEGE High School in Manhattan. There she was made to feel part of an elite, a Hunter girl, in a place where academic excellence set one apart.

Ozick describes this feeling fleetingly in the short story "An Education," in which Una Meyer excels in Latin, and in the long novel, *Trust*, contrasting the heroine's fruitful academic experience with her mother's empty-headed schooling at Miss Jewett's finishing school.

In a reminiscence she entitled "Washington Square, 1946," she tells how, eager for the new life awaiting her in college, she arrived a day early at the as yet unpopulated and therefore desolate campus of Washington Square College of New York University in Greenwich Village. In the Village, she discovers a newsstand that carries the *Partisan Review*, the journal of the literary avant-garde. Ozick will purchase her first non-textbook-book and browse through the Village's secondhand bookstores with the literary longing of youth. She will become a writer.

But first she would have to become an "old man." On graduation from college, Ozick set out for Columbus, Ohio, where, at Ohio State University, she pursued a graduate degree in English literature, earning a master's degree with the thesis "Parable in the Later Novels of Henry James." As she confesses in "The Lesson of the Master," she "became Henry James." In the title story of Ozick's 2008 collection of stories, *Dictation, Ozick imagines, for the metaphysical and literary fun of it, a literary hoax played on Henry James. Ozick's 2010 novel,* Foreign Bodies, *a masterpiece in its own right, has been taken by critics as a recasting of Henry James's masterpiece,* The Ambassadors. Most of Ozick's novel takes place in the Paris of 1952. The city is buzzing with literary-minded American expatriates seeking to sip espresso with Jean-Paul Sartre at Les Deux Magots. But Paris is pullulating with another type of foreign body: the refugees and displaced persons of the recent European Jewish cataclysm. The novel thus portrays what will become a familiar Ozick confrontation—the artist's desire place herself squarely in the wild fomenting atmosphere of literary creativity with Ozick's nagging need for a feeling of Jewish communal responsibility, in this case to give voice to the place of Jewish tragedy in real life. In her earlier essay, Ozick explains how she was influenced by Henry James to become a worshiper of literature, one who, having to choose between ordinary human entanglement—real life—and exclusive devotion to art, chooses art. She chose art over life, she says, to her eternal regret. Ozick asserts that she acted on the teaching of her mentor at the wrong time, while still a youth. It is not clear, however, that she did in fact abandon *la vraie vie,* as Proust puts it, for, at the age of twenty-four, in 1952, she married Bernard Hallote.

Upon receiving his degree, he would become a lawyer for the city of New York.

It is true, nevertheless, that during the first thirteen years of her marriage Ozick devoted herself exclusively to what she called "High Art," working on a philosophical novel, *Mercy, Pity, Peace, and Love,* called "MPPL" for short. Ozick would abandon this effort after several years, "a long suck on that Mippel," she would remark wryly. She also spent six and a half years, from 1957 to 1963, on *Trust,* another massive novel, published in 1966.

Ozick underwent a cultural transformation during that time. She became a Jewish autodidact, mastering for herself much of the Jewish textual tradition. Having read, at age twenty-five, Leo Baeck's "Romantic Religion," an essay that "seemed to decode the universe for me," she was further influenced, by Heinrich Graetz's *History of the Jews,* to add a Jewish nuance to *Trust.*

By becoming a "Jewish writer," Ozick did not abandon the world. But she did begin to wrestle with the term "Jewish writer." In 1965, the same year her daughter Rachel—today a Ph.D. in biblical archaeology—was born, she published several poems on Jewish themes in *Judaism* and produced "The Pagan Rabbi," published in 1966. She also wrote a hilarious short story based loosely on the career of Isaac Bashevis Singer, "Envy; or Yiddish in America," published in *Commentary* in 1969.

Her stature grew quickly. Three of her stories have won first prize in the O. Henry competition, and five of her stories were chosen for republication in the yearly anthologies of *Best American Short Stories.* The editor of the 1984 volume called her one of the three greatest American writers of stories living today. She was nominated for the National Book Award and the PEN/Faulkner Award and won half a dozen coveted awards and grants, including both a Guggenheim and a National Endowment for the Arts Fellowship. She was also given the precious commodity of time in the form of the American Academy of Arts and Letters Mildred and Harold Strauss Living Award for five years to pursue her craft. She has received several honorary doctorates and was invited to deliver the Phi Beta Kappa Oration at Harvard University. In 1986, she was the first recipient of the Michael Rea Award for career contributions to the short story. In 2000 she received the Lannan Foundation's Literary Award for Fiction.

After *Trust,* Ozick shied away from the novel, publishing at regular intervals *The Pagan Rabbi and Other Stories* (1971), *Bloodshed and Three Novellas* (1976), and *Levitation: Five Fictions* (1982). She returned to the novel quirkily, as the result of the settlement of a threatened lawsuit by a Jewish day school headmaster who had read himself, justifiably or not, into the 1980 short story, "The Laughter of Akiva." That story, enlarged and completely rewritten, became the novel *The Cannibal Galaxy* (1983). Another novel, *The Messiah of Stockholm* (1987), is sandwiched between two volumes of essays, *Art and Ardor* (1983) and *Metaphor and Memory* (1989). A third volume of essays, *Fame and Folly*, containing pieces on T.S. Eliot, Anthony Trollope, and Isaac Babel, was published in 1996. Meanwhile, in England, an essay collection called *Portrait of the Artist as a Bad Character* has been published.

Of Ozick's fascinating female characters—from Sheindel, the *sheytl-*wearing *rebbetzin* [bewigged rabbi's wife] in "The Pagan Rabbi," to Hester Lilt, the "imagistic linguistic logician" of *The Cannibal Galaxy*, to Rosa, the bag-lady Holocaust survivor of "The Shawl"—none is more beloved by admiring readers than Ruth Puttermesser, the protean heroine of Ozick's 1997 novel, *The Puttermesser Papers*. At first glance, one would characterize Puttermesser neither as heroine nor as beloved. She certainly would not be taken as a role model in either of the worlds to which she clings: the legal profession and the Jewish community, writ large. Most likely modeled on Ozick's lawyer-husband as much as on the writer herself, Ozick's Puttermesser is beloved for her intelligent and exemplary readings of the Jewish textual tradition, for her practical involvement in the repair of the world, and for her ability to mingle the law with the lore. She is beloved because, although she is finally defeated, like all of us, by entropy, she teaches, by example, that every innocuous butter knife (the meaning of *Puttermesser*) can cut through life to its core of meaning. As Ozick stated in a piece published in a special edition of *Life* magazine on "The Meaning of Life," "Our task is to clothe nature, ... to impose meaning on being.... Our task is the discipline of standing against nature when nature-within-us counsels terrorizing.... Our task is to invent civilization."

That is Puttermesser speaking, but it is also Rosa. In 1980, Ozick published, in the *New Yorker*, "The Shawl," two thousand words of finely honed impressionism, a rendering in miniature of the Holocaust in all its horror. A movingly dramatic reading of "The Shawl" by actress CLAIRE BLOOM was featured in 1995 on *Jewish Short Stories from Eastern Europe and Beyond*, a National Public Radio series subsequently published on audiocassette by the National Yiddish Book Center. In 1983, again in the *New Yorker,* Ozick published a sequel to "The Shawl," expanding it into "Rosa," a novella whose heft permitted her publisher to issue *The Shawl* (1989) as a separate volume, consisting of the story and the novella. Probably the most widely accessible of Ozick's demanding prose works, it is now found on the reading lists of most college courses on the literature of the Holocaust, along with works by Elie Wiesel and Primo Levi. Ozick told the *Paris Review* in an interview that she would prefer not to make art out of the Holocaust. "I don't want to tamper or invent or imagine, and yet I have done it. I can't not do it. It comes. It invades." She moved from the modern paradigm of suffering to its ancient counterpart in her preface to the *The Book of Job* (1998), in which she examines the linguistic, narrative and philosophical elements of the Biblical work.

If the Holocaust has invaded Ozick's consciousness—it is present in different guises in "The Pagan Rabbi," "Levitation," The Messiah of Stockholm and Foreign Bodies as well—all the more so has the ugly phenomenon of Holocaust denial invaded her conscience. In an article in the Washington Post Book World (January 15, 1995), explaining how she came to write the play Blue Light (1994), she relates how, as early as 1961, she came to realize that the world had attenuated the Holocaust into the "Second World War," as though Zyklon B, the deadly gas used to murder Jews, were nothing more than an artifact of war. The road from attenuation to revisionism to Holocaust denial became an increasingly simple one for her to trace.

During her fifth decade as a writer, Ozick became what she has called an "elderly novice." She had long before promised herself that she would one day write for the theater. Eager to wallow in the "delectable theatrical dark," she decided in 1990 to dramatize for the stage "The Shawl" and "Rosa." The play was originally scheduled to be produced by Robert Brustein at the American Repertory Theatre in Cambridge, Massachusetts. Ozick did several rewrites—making the figure of the denier more and more "satanic"—but the production was canceled for budgetary reasons. In 1992, after more revisions, the play received two staged readings in New York at Playwrights Horizons. Its first full-blown production, under the direction of Sidney Lumet, took place at Sag Harbor's Bay Street Theatre. Finally, after fifteen or so revisions, *The Shawl* was produced off-Broadway, at Playhouse 91 of the American Jewish Repertory Theatre, in 1996.

Given Ozick's stature in the literary world, the play received considerable critical attention. Ben Brantley, reviewing it in the *New York Times* (June 21, 1996), was awed by Ozick's power "to let us temporarily, but thoroughly, inhabit someone else's mind." What Brantley missed, however, was Ozick's intention "not to be merciful to the cruel," that is, to the Holocaust deniers.

Although Ozick has only good things to say about Sidney Lumet and the other theater people she has worked with, she has expressed regret that she had to spend so much time on the mechanics and staging of this play, time that otherwise might have been spent "breathing inside a blaze of words," practicing the solitary art of the prose writer. Her recent return to the essay and to prose fiction marks yet another beginning for Ozick, and the product is as fresh as the work of a young experimental novelist. Witness her entry into cyberspace in the fall of 1996 with a ten-day "Diary" on Michael Kinsley's Internet magazine *Slate*. (In the "Diary," Ozick reveals that she has been keeping a private diary since 1953, when she was twenty-five years old.)

She returned to questions of the Holocaust—including "Who Owns Anne Frank?"—and other issues in her 2001 book of essays *Quarrel and Quandary*, which won the National Book Critics Circle Award for criticism. Ozick suggests that the Holocaust is almost—but not quite—resistant to the literary efforts to encompass it. She is particularly angered by the morphing of Frank's diary into Broadway-style cheerfulness, a transformation that "tampers with history, with reality, with deadly truth."

In 2001 she received the Guardian of Zion Award from Bar-Ilan University "in recognition of her contribution to literature; and in particular, in recognition of her spirited defense of the Jewish People and Zionism in her non-fiction writing and public speaking."

Ozick had pieces on *The Portrait of a Lady* and GERTRUDE STEIN, as well as a fictional account of a visit from a Muscovite cousin published in her regular outlets, the *New York Times Book Review*, the *New York Times Magazine,* and the *New Yorker*. Telling much about the heights that she reaches in American literature today, in 1997 the *New Yorker* published a major essay by Ozick on Dostoyevsky. Posterity will judge whether Fyodor and Shoshana-Cynthia are playing in the same Garden.

SELECTED WORKS BY CYNTHIA OZICK

Art and Ardor (1983); *Bloodshed and Three Novellas* (1976); *Blue Light* (1994); *The Book of Job,* preface by Cynthia Ozick (1998); *A Cynthia Ozick Reader* (1996); *Dictation (2008); Fame and Folly* (1996); *The Cannibal Galaxy* (1983); *Foreign Bodies (2010); Heir to the Glimmering World: A Novel* (2004); *Levitation: Five Fictions* (1982); *The Messiah of Stockholm* (1987); *Metaphor and Memory* (1989); *The Pagan Rabbi and Other Stories* (1971); *The Puttermesser Papers* (1997); *Quarrel and Quandary: Essays* (2001); *The Shawl* (play) (1996); *The Shawl: A Story and Novella* (1989); *Trust* (1966).

REFERENCES

Currier, Susan, and Daniel J. Cahill. "A REFERENCES of the Writings of Cynthia Ozick." *Texas Studies in Literature and Language* 25, no. 2 (Summer 1983): 313–321; Lowin, Joseph. *Cynthia Ozick* (1988); Moyers, Bill. "Heritage Conversation with Cynthia Ozick." Transcript, WNET-TV, New York, April 3, 1986; Teicholz, Tom. "[*Paris Review* Interview with] Cynthia Ozick." *Paris Review* 102 (Spring 1987): 154–190; Kauver, Elaine M. *Cynthia Ozick's Fiction: Tradition and Invention* (1993); Cohen, Sarah Blacher. *Cynthia Ozick's Comic Art: From Levity to Liturgy* (1994); Marcus, James. "Quarrel and Quandary: Essays." *Twentieth Century History Books.com,* 2001.

Dr. Joseph Lowin was most recently director of the National Center for the Hebrew Language. Previously, Lowin was director of Cultural Services at the National Foundation for Jewish Culture, the Midrasha Institute of Adult Jewish Studies, and Adult Jewish Education at Hadassah. A Ph.D. from Yale University, Lowin has held faculty appointments at Yale, the University of Miami and Touro College. He has been a Fulbright Fellow at the Sorbonne and a Jerusalem Fellow. Lowin has published more than 100 essays and reviews on Jewish literature as well as a book on the literary universe of Cynthia Ozick. He is currently at work on a book about art and creativity in the contemporary Israeli novel, forthcoming from Lexington Books (Rowman and Littlefield).

3. With James and Ozick in Paris: The Ambassadors and Foreign Bodies

Sanford Marovitz

On looking through the reviews of *Foreign Bodies* shortly after its publication in 2010, at least some readers were likely to be surprised that many of those critiques begin with reference not to Ozick's novel but to Henry James's *The Ambassadors* (1903). Or James's novel may be mentioned significantly in the opening paragraph as the one that the author himself had assessed as "frankly, quite the best 'all round,' of all my productions" (James, "Preface," 8), an evaluation with which many of his current readers still agree, including Ozick herself. Clearly, the reviewers, took advantage of the author's relating her new novel to James's classic by highlighting the association with it from the start.

As she had written in several essays, Ozick had been psychologically captivated by James as a graduate student aspiring to be a master author at the same high level that he had reached over decades of experience particularly as a writer of fiction, but she intended to achieve this worthy goal in a few years at most. With that in mind, she spent months working toward her broad target date, many of them in "the black hole of a microfilm cell" studying for her Master's Degree and transcribing letters he had written to his agent in London, J. B. Pinker, until ultimately she acknowledged, "I had become Henry James, and for years and years I remained Henry James" (Ozick, "The Lesson of the Master" *Art & Ardor*, 293-4). Drafting what became her first published novel, *Trust* (1966), she kept on her writing table as a "talisman" a worn copy of *The Ambassadors*, which she had already admired for years, and ultimately she returned to that extraordinary narrative to employ it as a means of integrating it with her own work-in-progress, *Foreign Bodies*, by basing its plot on James's.

Essentially, the story in both novels begins when a parent sends an associate or family member to Paris in order to retrieve an unwilling son who was to return home a few years earlier but has apparently decided to remain abroad indefinitely without explanation. In both cases an older woman is assumed to be the reason for the young man's delayed return, and that supposition is partly confirmed. If the plots are similar, the characters, major and minor, are not, yet to an extent their roles correspond. Decidedly different from parallels that exist in the plots, however, are the novels' temporal settings—and that is a signal distinction. Although both are set chiefly in Paris, a little over half the twentieth century separates them in terms of time, and two world wars brought changes to the city that could not have been imagined when James was composing *The Ambassadors*.

Therefore, it should be helpful to readers of the two novels to keep in mind a kind of stereoscopic version of the city that exhibits Paris during these different time periods. One view, from the closing decade of the nineteenth century through the first one and a half of the twentieth; a second view from the 1920s through the mid-1930s; and a third from that point through the first three years of the 1950s. This tri-optic vision of the city would enable readers to stand beside Lambert Strether, then, the central consciousness of *The Ambassadors*, from his arrival in London through his stay in Paris, which began soon after he had entered the city and ended with his departure about three months later. The second optic view would display Paris as imagined and often experienced by artists, authors, musicians, students, and tourists, especially but not only Americans, all eager to see and perhaps enjoy in a limited way the city they had heard and read so much about during the preceding and current decades. The third and final view would then exhibit Paris in the early 1950s, in many ways a very different city after World War Two when young American travelers thinking in terms of the "Lost Generation" were still arriving, while countless survivors, especially of the *Shoah*, had gravitated there from elsewhere in Europe, often from farther east, seeking new lives outside the former war zone.

These three views would display first, the way James himself saw and experienced Paris during his many visits there; the second would exhibit the way that Americans and others of the next generation envisioned it when Hemingway, Fitzgerald, Gertrude Stein, Picasso, Virgil Thomson, Stravinsky, James Joyce, Gershwin, and dozens of other famous figures in the arts were in and out of that "vast bright Babylon" as Julian Nachtigall, the recalcitrant son in *Foreign Bodies*, had doubtlessly imagined it. But Julian initially attempts to make a life there for himself, although by that time, the twenties and early thirties he had sought in Paris, were long gone. Yet he stays, writing in his notebook, eating whatever leftovers he can scrape from the café dishes and tables he clears when his money is gone. Eventually, he is observed by Lili, a Romanian survivor of the Nazis, Fascists, and Communists, and she takes him over; her surname remains unknown. Ozick said in an interview the year that *Foreign Bodies* was published that she had not wanted or intended to write another survival novel, but "Julian goes to Paris looking for the mythic Europe that the Lost Generation [of the 1920s] so glamorized, and he finds this Holocaust survivor. I don't [sic] want to deal with another survivor," she said to Jane Ciabattari in an interview, but "Lili is just there. I couldn't help it. That is Europe" (Ciabattari, "Mad for HJ," *Book Beast* [11/15/10]; www, *Daily Beast*, com. "Cynthia Ozick interview: HJ and Foreign Bodies," html).

Among several other survivors she might have had in mind from her earlier fiction are those in particular she had portrayed in "The Shawl," *Rosa*, and *The Messiah of Stockholm*, the most important of which for insight into *Foreign Bodies* is "The Shawl," the first and shortest of these titles [1980, no more than a few pages without the accompanying *Rosa* nine years later]. In a death camp Rosa had been hiding Magda, her toddler, under a shawl while nursing her with dry breasts and only the corner of her worn shawl to suck on. When the prisoners are all in the yard, Magda dashes unexpectedly from the barracks on her spindly legs; quickly she is picked up and lifted overhead by a guard, and thrown high against the electric fence that sizzles as it catches and burns the flying child to cinders. Fearing for her own life, Rosa stands transfixed and silent as she watches the remains of her daughter drop like shards to the ground. After their liberation, she and her niece, Stella, who had been imprisoned with her in the camp, eventually find their way to the U.S., where they open a small store in New York City. Rosa's bitter departure from there to Miami immediately follows her trashing the store in anger, and she soon becomes disgusted in Florida over her initially incomprehensible new life there as an immigrant receiving but limited support from Stella.

Clearly her early days in Florida are less than promising as described in the novelette *Rosa* published in 1989 with "The Shawl" reprinted as a prologue.

Ultimately, however, Rosa comes to terms with the degraded life-style she perceives while wandering around Miami observing poverty on the streets and in the shops of her neighborhood, the low-class but hospitable hotel where she has a room, and gay men enjoying their evening half-buried together in the warm beach sand of a luxury hotel where she is quietly prompted to leave by the management. She remains hostile to the numerous requests she receives in the mail for interviews and statements as a Holocaust survivor. Before long, however, she becomes acquainted with Simon Persky, who befriends and successfully "coaxes her," as Sarah Blacher Cohen expresses it, "to choose life" over chronic distress and bitterness (*Cynthia Ozick's Comic Art,* 171). She also gains psychological assistance from memories of her small daughter, Magda, who still lives in her consciousness as a successful young woman to whom Rosa writes daily letters in her native Polish to keep her child alive for her own sanity. "Fortunately," Cohen adds, "in Ozick's best work"—and "The Shawl" exemplifies it—"there is an agile dialectic between the comic and the sacred, a deft integration between levity and liturgy" (173). She might have added a touch of sentimentality as well to this moving statement because it is surely applicable.

Three years after the publication of her extended version of "The Shawl" appeared in 1989 Ozick brought out *The Messiah of Stockholm* (1987), a highly satirical novel in which Lars Andemening, like James's Lambert Strether, is both protagonist and central consciousness, but that is the only meaningful correspondence between those two principal figures. Completely ignorant of his heritage, including the name he received at his birth in Poland, Lars emigrated to Sweden shortly after World War Two and selected a surname for himself from a dictionary in his adoptive land—Andemening ("inward meaning")—and made no reference then to his being a Jew (Cohen, 131). According to Ozick, he "understood about himself" that he was the son of Bruno Schulz and "was still in his mother's womb" when his already legendary father was shot and killed (*Messiah,* 4) by a Nazi SS man outside the ghetto of Drohobycz, the diminutive Galician city in southeastern Poland, where he lived and taught art in the high school. Although Lars never knew his mother's name, Ozick says, "his father had become his craze" (*Messiah,*

4). Ozyck does not explain why Lars "understood" that his murdered father was Bruno Schulz but only that he had developed a passion to learn all he could about his assumed father. Probably because of this obsession over his father, she says that Lars "shrank himself: all [Schulz's] tales were about men shrinking more and more into the phantasmagoria of the mind" (Ozick, 51). Consequently, Lars chose to review only the big, esoteric publications of Central Europe, unlike his colleagues who sought popularity for their reviews; although he would have preferred more attention, Lars was slow about changing.

Early in the novel Gunnar Hemlig, a colleague reviewer in the "Stewpot" (i.e., the editorial office for the *Morgontörn*) and reputedly "an authority on the American novel" (*Messiah*, 13), cautions Lars that his readers are few because he is "a beautiful soul" and that "a daily reviewer shouldn't be a beautiful soul. It leads to belles-lettres, which leads to exultation and other forms of decline" (13). Eventually, Lars heeds this advice toward celebrating mediocrity in his reviews after becoming involved in a confidence game controlled by Dr. Ecklund (né Eckstein) and his wife, Heidi, refugees trying to make a living however they can, underhanded or not. Lars had become acquainted with Heidi through her used-book store not far from the *Morgontörn* building; she helps him find what she says are authentic original publications of his assumed father, but some if not all of those she located were fraudulent—manufactured by her husband and sold to Lars. When Adela, who claims to be Bruno Schulz's daughter, brings what she asserts is the original manuscript of *The Messiah* to Lars's apartment for him to see, he rejects both her insistence that she is his sister and that the manuscript is authentic. Nevertheless when he struggles to seize it from her, she flees with the alleged manuscript in a white sack. The next day she appears at the bookstore, where Heidi, her husband, and Lars have already congregated, the sack having been emptied into a brass amphora. She claims to have recovered it from Warsaw and Drohobycz, where it had been hidden by its presumably Jewish owners before they fled from the Nazis. Sometime earlier the manuscript had been torn into many pieces, but Lars has enough time to put parts of it together and read it well enough to make sense of the complicated symbolic narrative in which much is burned and many idolatrous beings are sacrificed by a Messianic creature that has only a momentary existence but creates a small, weak bird with a piece of straw in its beak that it uses to douse the fires on individual idols before the brief Messianic narrative ends. In his review of *The Messiah of Stockholm*, Sanford Pinsker suggests that Ozick herself would likely acknowledge "the essential Jewishness of her vision, but . . . one will have to look deeper than the work of Bruno Schulz . . . to find appropriate analogues. My own hunch is that Kabbalah explains much of the energy in *The Messiah of Stockholm*" (Pinsker, 60). Perhaps the piece of straw has touched Lars himself, who has been considering for some time taking another name—"Baruch Lazarus"—and reclaiming his Jewish heritage and identity, but by the end of the novel he has not officially made such a change.

Yet Lars's story is still not quite finished. Seven months after the burning of the manuscript, having readjusted his life by reviewing mediocre books and acquiring a larger, more favorable reading audience, Lars lives normally in a satisfactory apartment furnished with modern utilities and comforts where he is visited in his larger office by the former Adela and her son of about six years. Among other things, she has come to tell Lars that he had been "used," that the burned manuscript had been authentic, the only one in existence, and that the guilt is his. Ozick appears to have left it up to her readers to decide if she has told him the truth, but she has gone beyond that question to end the novel with a short chapter that evokes a melancholy feeling in Lars that implies he may not be altogether happy over replacing his formerly honest, insightful reviews with mediocrity for the sake of popularity.

A brief concluding paragraph recalls these questions about Lars's deep feelings over being "used" by "a pack of swindlers" *(Messiah,* 128), over the chance he took of destroying the only true manuscript of Schulz's *Messiah*, over the possible truth of the way Adela described her recovery of it after it was saved from destruction in Warsaw and Drohobycz by men in black coats ferrying it in long garter boxes to protect it, as well as over the loss of his young daughter to his divorced wife who had taken her to the U.S. and settled there, and finally over his lack of family and warm friendships in a foreign land. All of these concerns and memories remain with him even after his rewarding transformation into modernity. Only perhaps as a lingering result of such disturbing thoughts that occasionally return "in the blue light of Stockholm . . . he grieved" (144). With this poignant sentence near the end of Ozick's ambiguous satire, she reveals her enduring admiration and appreciation of Bernard Malamud's subtle insight into Jewish melancholy as she unexpectedly transforms the pleasure Lars has gained from his recent public approval to his grief as a mourner. (See Ozick, Cynthia, "Judging the World: Library of America's Bernard Malamud Collections," *NYTBR* [*3/16/14*], 1ff, for an account of her deep appreciation for Malamud.)

By the time that her next major novel appeared in 2010 nearly a quarter century had passed. *Foreign Bodies* is a more profound and serious novel than *The Messiah of Stockholm* as well as vastly broader in geographical coverage, its overall setting extending from Romania to Southern California with focal locations in Los Angeles, New York City, and Paris. Although not lacking in satire, its humor in most instances is considerably darker, exhibiting aspects of Bruno Schulz's art and imagery in its descriptions. An exception to this generalization opens early in Ozick's more recent novel and is richly developed several chapters later. In these segments, Ozick returns to the duplicity theme recurrent throughout *The Messiah of Stockholm* with the many references to forgery, false identities, and to the *Morgontörn* reviewers celebrating mediocrity instead of literary value or sound information. In *Foreign Bodies*, Julian, the derelict son of Marvin Nachtigall, takes advantage of an offer to live rent free in a large apartment that serves as the Parisian clinic for a quack doctor Julian had met, an allegedly practicing physician whose only curative skills are creating liniments and lotions from vegetables and having false professional cards printed and distributed. Dr. Phillip Montalbano (he took the name from that of an admirable Italian village he had passed through during the war) has several such clinics across Europe and carries on a highly successful business. These humorous passages help tie *Foreign Bodies* to the satire in much of Ozick's earlier fiction, including *The Cannibal Galaxy* (1983) and *The Puttermesser Papers* (1997) as well as *The Messiah of Stockholm*, and others.

Paris in the summer of 1952 was still suffering from the massive population shift that had begun several years earlier, less than a decade after its liberation from the Vichy government and the Nazis as the war was ending. Large numbers of East-European refugees, especially Jewish survivors of the *Shoah*, still roamed within the city seeking not only a way out of it but one that offered a promise of security, a welcome with some assurance of employment after their arrival. It was a miserably hot, humid summer in Paris that year, which made urban living amid crowds of largely destitute foreigners especially uncomfortable. This was particularly true for the Jews, the vast majority of whom by far had lost whatever they had owned before the war and ventured to Paris hoping that the government might help them locate inhabitants of other countries, perhaps in the Americas, who may be related to them or otherwise be situated in a position to help them fulfill their intense desire to leave France and emigrate to some nation that would prove hospitable and compatible.

With respect to *The Ambassadors* and *Foreign Bodies*, the basic resemblance in their plots—retrieving a reluctant young man in Paris and returning him to his family in the United States—appears simple enough on the face of it, but the likeness of the two stories is complicated by the differences in the young men's character and the temporal settings, i.e., the nature of the actions in relation to completely different circumstances. What should not be minimized in relating the two novels is a devastating experience that occurs in the life of the principal figure in each—Strether and Lili—both of whom have lost a spouse and child. Strether's young family died of illness many years before, a loss strangely unmentioned by James in the "Preface" to his novel, yet it was serious enough to have left Strether himself bereft, feeling as though the meaning of his own life had bottomed out before he would come back to Paris years later as the first "ambassador" his unofficial fiancée has sent to bring her lackadaisical son, Chad, back home. Lili, in contrast, lost her family during the war period when her husband, son, and both parents were shot; somehow she escaped with an ugly, gaping bullet wound disfiguring her arm and made her way to France. Not long after Strether has returned to Paris on this mission for Mrs. Newsome, however, his life gains new meaning when he sees how Chad has benefited from living amid a bright, wealthy community of international socialites in the city with a charming and youthful-appearing countess, Mme. de Vionnet, at its center, and her equally engaging young daughter, Jeanne, at her side. In consequence, Strether soon becomes captivated by the life he finds there, sophisticated but not exclusive, and the longer he stays through the spring and much of the summer, the more difficult he finds it to lure Chad away and restore him to his mother. However, it is also worth noting that as time passes he sympathizes increasingly with Chad's immersion in the social and intellectual milieu of Mme. de Vionnet that appears to have been of such benefit in sophisticating the young man to a level that has proved so surprising to Strether that remembering the loss of his own wife and small son no longer holds the same dominating influence over his desire to live fully as it had only a few weeks earlier. He had first arrived in Paris then and conveyed to John Little Bilham, a young American member of the group, the importance of living a rich full life before age squelches the opportunity as he initially believes it did his own: "Live all you can; it's a mistake not to. It doesn't so much matter what you do in particular, so long as you have your life. If you haven't had that, what *have* you had?... Don't miss things out of stupidity.... Do what you like as long as you don't make my mistake. For it was a mistake. Live!" (James, 21: 217-18.)

Before leaving Paris, however, he seems to reconsider what had apparently been a foregone conclusion. But ultimately he is stricken by a revelation by Mme. de Vionnet near the close of the novel when she breaks down and informs him that she is deathly afraid of aging and dying as an old woman; she wants desperately to remain young. Strether is stunned. His disappointment over hearing this brilliant woman break down over such a fear is very difficult for him to accommodate, and already disillusioned over learning that her relation with Chad was not the "virtuous attachment" (James, 21: 180, 202) he had been advised it was, further uncertainty over remaining in Paris longer than necessary has been resolved for him. Beyond that, for James, Strether's advice to Bilham constitutes the essential message of the novel ("Preface," v), and a return to Woollett appears to be equally out of the question.

Early in *The Ambassadors*, Strether is unknowingly introduced to what will be for him an altogether unfamiliar way of life when he meets and speaks for the first time with Maria Gostrey in England shortly before leaving for Paris; she is to be his principal fi☐elle (confidante) in France. Soon after his arrival there he will become acquainted with Chad Newsome, the young man he has agreed to find and return to his mother, the wealthy Mrs. Newsome, in Woollett. It is understood by both Mrs. Newsome and her "ambassador" that whatever his intention to remain in Paris may be, it is likely that extended time will be necessary to convince Chad to return because they assume that he would probably not have remained in Paris without a compelling reason. By the time the novel ends, the early intentions and expectations seem to have completely turned around, and it appears that without attempting to formulate other plans before he leaves his new acquaintances behind in Paris and probably older ones in Woollett, Strether seems prepared to seek an independent life much on the order of what he had encouraged little Bilham to do.

Whereas James's novel may be perceived as constructed less like an extended work of fiction than as the precise account of a perceptive and imaginative observer in an engaging new environment with Strether at the center, Ozick's *Foreign Bodies* incorporates several tangentially related stories in progress simultaneously. Each has its own center, and Marvin Nachtigall as father, brother, husband, and inestimably wealthy manufacturer of plastic airplane parts has some causative role in all of them, but he lacks real control over his family, all of whom largely act independently to the extent possible, leaving him to think of himself as a power base, which he actually is not because his fortune, enormous as it is, does not control anything beyond himself and his own business. His sister, Beatrice, and his unwelcome daughter-in-law, Lili, whom he has never met nor wished to meet, are controllers in the best sense, especially Lili before Beatrice begins to act on her own to influence younger members of the Nachtigall family, notably Iris (Julian's older sister), as well as Julian himself. Ultimately after observing Lili's unexpected strengths and capabilities, Bea assumes more responsibility for both Julian and his wife even before they leave for the U.S and arrive at her apartment door in New York amidst nasty winter weather at its worst. Until then and after, his father futilely and unknowingly insists that his son return from Paris and resume his studies after neglecting them for three years, but Julian remains inaccessible to him.

Marvin's wife, Margaret, from an exclusive Protestant family, is the sister of his former room-mate at Princeton; he had conned her into asserting her independence in an anti-Semitic household and marrying a Jew; she was adventuresome and open-minded but unfortunate in choosing the wrong Jew to wed. After over two decades of marriage, she remains independent only within the limits of the luxurious Suite Eyre Spa in Beverly Hills where she is confined by her own choice, as she tells Beatrice during a surprise visit; Marvin, however, although not present when her remarks are made, disagrees with that notion, insisting that he had arranged to have her admitted for observation and care as a mental patient because she was sleeping all the time, and she concurred with his plan. After visiting and speaking with her there without Marvin's knowledge, Beatrice finds her quickly responsive in conversation and does not yet believe that anything is wrong with Margaret's mind, but her flight from the spa when an opportunity occurs, an "escape" that leads to her death when she is hit by a bus on a busy highway near the sanitarium, would seem to confirm Marvin's appraisal. Equally persuasive, however, are Margaret's paintings. Although Julian tells Lili that he had never heard his mother speak of paintings, she has been provided with the necessary materials and tools to learn how to draw and paint at the Suite Eyre. When Beatrice visits her studio, she senses an awful stench as she approaches Margaret's easel and perceives that Marvin's wife—i.e., her own sister-in-law—has "mastered the art of human excrement" (95).

Whereas the emphasis of *The Ambassadors* is on a combination of perception and imagination in the mind of Lambert Strether, the chief stress in *Foreign Bodies* is on Julian Nachtigall's struggle to break free of his wealthy father's sustained attempt to regain control of him. With respect to Lili in Ozick's novel, however, who has suffered a loss similar to Strether's but attributable to war and violence rather than a natural cause, she turns to Julian almost immediately after meeting him by chance in an outdoor Parisian café apparently because she believes that she can help him. Lili, in contrast to Strether, lost her family during the war period when her husband, son, and both parents were shot in Transistria or Romania; perhaps with God's help she escaped with a large, ugly bullet-wound distorting her arm and found her way to Paris. Her own small family is dead and gone amid the ravages of Eastern Europe, and although it is evident at times that they remain deeply ensconced in her memory and heart, they are long past aid that she or anyone can provide. Julian, however, seems to her a floundering soul who can use guidance but has little to offer in exchange for it. She observes him as a slovenly, gross, laughable youth from somewhere other than France attempting unsuccessfully to write something in his notebook that he has but vaguely in mind. "Damn, I can't do it," he says aloud; she looks up, perceives his despair, and suddenly encourages him by responding, "Then you must persist" (*FB,* 100). She sympathizes with him possibly because she senses something in him—maybe a faint resemblance to her own son slain in his twenties (*FB,* 104)—that suggests compassion and perhaps promise for the two of them, and they leave together. In any case, it is clearly an act of *Tikkun,* the Hebrew word for redemption, "the restoration of harmony" that was lost, according to the Kabbalists, when the divine light of creativity shattered the shells meant to hold it (Scholem, *Maj. Tr.,* 233; *On the Kab.,* 112-13).

It is as if Lili had a mystical insight that remains unstated but seems real for them both. Although the situation at the outset appears vastly different from that in *The Ambassadors*, where Chad has acquired such social grace among the well-to-do Parisian coterie that has welcomed him, at least three basic similarities moderate the difference. First, soon after meeting each other, both Lili and Julian show devotion and caring to the extent that they marry and live together on whatever money they can muster. Second, Julian desperately needs to be cared for, and Lili is gracious and loving as she accommodates him; and third, Lili has the strength that Julian lacks, a strength that enables her to work toward satisfying the needs of them both, needs that she can perceive but he cannot. At times it is more than the lack of adequate money because Julian still occasionally if rarely receives checks from his extremely wealthy father. When that money runs out, Lili's pittance of an income for her work as a translator in the Refugee Center does not provide for them both. Fortunately for Julian, Lili has a limited command of several languages as well as somewhat more than a knowledge of basic English; in addition, she learns fast and immediately puts to effective, practical use whatever new knowledge she acquires. She also consents to be Julian's sex partner on demand, including on an occasion only a few hours after she had suffered through a clinical abortion that she had found necessary and still remains extremely painful; she quietly allows Julian—who knows no better—to pull her to him for sex notwithstanding the agony it causes her. He seems unaware of it, and she never complains (178).

Not until long after meeting him does she learn vaguely about the trouble-laden wealth of his father's broken Nachtigall family in the United States, and by then or very soon after, she has committed herself to Julian by becoming his wife and suffering with him. As Carole S. Kessner observes in her excellent historical study of this novel, an understanding of Lili's strengths ultimately makes clear to Beatrice, who learns much from Julian's wife, that she "has been a brisk force for change for those whose lives she touches" (Kessner, 213). Of course, Lili learns much as well from Beatrice, who has been teaching spirited high-school boys successfully in New York City for decades; having gained their respect through her success as their instructor and sensible disciplinarian over that extended period of time, Julian's Aunt Bea is a good source of information on many aspects of American life, and Lili takes fair advantage of it.

Apart from Marvin, Beatrice is the most independent individual in *Foreign Bodies*, although she does not assert her individuality until she begins to disobey her brother's demands—and they *are* demands—but when she starts acting on her own as she thinks best, she simultaneously renders his powerful influence ineffective. While still in college she had married Leo Coopersmith, a student with aspirations toward becoming a major composer of symphonic music; after she graduates and becomes an English teacher to support his education at Julliard, they live in her one-room apartment in a six-story walk-up and share the room with a grand piano they had received as a wedding gift. They remain married for an unspecified few years until their divorce when he moves to the Los Angeles area still aspiring to become a prominent symphonist. It never happens, but after many years of accumulating and spending wealth as a successful musical-score writer for films, he finally sends Bea an original score for a full-length symphony he had just completed: "*The Nightingale's Thorn:* SYMPHONY IN B MINOR by Leo Coopersmith." Bea opens the package having no idea of what he has sent her; the pages drop and float all around her. The odd-looking musical symbols are incomprehensible to her, but she is giddy with happiness because Leo has sent her "a gift—a kind of gift. Leo's mind! It was the thing she had hoped for, long ago." She is elated over the gift, of course, and much stirred: "Her heart in its cage a foreign body" (FB, 253-4). She remembers one of his little jokes from years back: "Symphony in Bea Minor." The memories stir up a frenzy in her, and she is utterly thrilled. He has remained firmly in her mind since their divorce, and as Ozick infers in the closing sentence of the novel, "in the long, long war with Leo, wasn't it Bea who'd won?" (FB, 255.)

    What Bea does not know, however, is how important she was as an initiator of that composition because when she had visited him in his mansion not far from the Suite Eyre Spa where she had stopped to see Margaret, she was distressed to know that he had still composed no major work, not even on his grand piano there on which Gustav Mahler had written a symphony. The piano stands beside her. When he becomes upset over her comments, she lifts the lid over the keyboard and smashes the splayed fingers of her left hand down on the bass keys and her right fist down hard on the treble. "The sound was tremendous, the sound was august, it was a thunder, a chorus of tragical gods, it was out of the deeps, it was out of the sky, it was hail, it was it was flung stones, it was majesty! It was the opening bars of the symphony he was yet to write" (FB, 115). Since her visit long before, Leo had been attempting to reproduce the sound of those chords that Beatrice had pounded out until he finally did it. Will he go beyond them and his new B-Minor Symphony? No, in this novel, he will not.

Beatrice is the only member of the Nachtigall family who has exchanged her German (not Yiddish) name for the English Nightingale, which is easier for her students to pronounce (and lightly tease her about); not even Marvin has made that change. No one else in the family can understand why, although it appears to be further evidence of his silently acknowledging that he is a self-hating Jew. Margaret, his Protestant wife, cannot explain it, either; both she and her husband have been largely written off by her Breckinridge family, she for marrying a Jew, and he for being one. Perhaps she is quietly bitter about it herself, having been victimized by her choice. As Carole S. Kessner explains, Margaret's maiden name has strong anti-Semitic implications (210). During Bea's visit Margaret tells her candidly that her husband has assumed a new legacy by taking over her family's heraldic crest: "He's turned himself into what he thinks I am. That crest! . . . Can't you understand?" she asks Bea; "my husband has no existence! He doesn't exist. He has no self!" (*FB*, 92, 93).

Although little specific attention has been given thus far to the Jewish theme in *Foreign Bodies*, readers familiar with Ozick's essays and fiction may assume that Judaism has a prominent role in this novel as it does in most of her earlier writing. This should be evident initially from Lili's suffering and the destruction of her family as Jews during war. She also undoubtedly learns from Julian's Aunt Bea and his sister, Iris, when they come to Paris individually to find and possibly bring him home, that the Nachtigall family into which Julian's father, Marvin, was born were Eastern European immigrants who had maintained their Jewish faith, unlike their son. Furthermore, Lili is certain to have been informed that his father had married a Christian, and she understands that according to Hebrew law, Julian is not Jewish because the heritage is passed to the children only through the mother. Apparently with this in mind, Lili seems determined to establish her husband's affiliation with Judaism; thus far he lacks an understanding of such matters; he believes that he is "half a Jew" (*FB* 134) and seems but little interested in the question, declaring at one point that "only In the Psalms is God real, nowhere else" (177). But Lili knows better and encourages him to continue his "study"—i.e., reading and copying—of the Psalms; insisting that God exists only in the Psalms, Julian wishes to prove that God does not exist at all, and he is copying out the Psalms in his notebook with that aim in mind. Lili encourages him probably because she is sure that if he reads them intelligently, which she is certain he is learning to do, his interest and effort will be rewarded.

Lili is a quick study herself. She works hard, learns fast, and seems almost always to be correct in whatever she says and does. She is an altogether remarkable figure, perhaps as close to perfect under the circumstances as any mortal can be. But as an immortal figure, a quasi-mystical figure, as if endowed with the divine attributes of the *Shekhinah*, she is precisely the "true wife" that Julian needs to oversee his maturation and development as a Jew. She is a personification of strength, and their "true marriage," like all true marriages, "is a symbolical realization of the union of God and *Shekhinah*," according to Gershon Scholem (Scholem, *Maj. Tr.*, 235). Moreover, Scholem explains that "the earthly Community of Israel is formed after the archetype of the mystical Community of Israel which is the *Shekhinah*" (*Maj. Tr.*, 233). It is also important to note that the poverty to which Julian and Lili are often subject relates directly to the Psalms and the *Zohar*, which Scholem has concluded was written in Spain by Moses de Leon toward the end of the 13th century (*Zohar* 119). Further, he points out that the "glorification of poverty" in the biblical Psalms that so heavily engage Julian was "considerably dimmed" in the later rabbinical period until it brightened again about the time of the *Zohar (Maj. Tr.*, 234). Still more pertinent for associating Lili and Julian with the mystical significance of their poverty is Scholem's remark that "To the mystics, the poor are 'God's broken vessels'" (234), and the vessels must be restored to hold the divine light after the shells meant to hold it shattered upon impact.

Lili's escape from Axis, Fascist, and Communist controlled territory, then her appearance at an apt time for meeting Julian and marrying him soon after, and her leading him in the right direction regularly, especially toward restoring his affiliation with Judaism, further suggest that she has the support of divine aid to an extraordinary degree. Perhaps twice as old as Julian who is about twenty-three when they are married and worn down from suffering and grief, Lili hardly seems divine in herself, yet Ozick has perhaps inadvertently given her the special features that appear to have God's touch behind them. With this and more in her favor, it is not difficult to make a strong case for Lili (of the Valley) with the support of Rose (of Sharon) in her background as representing the mystical figure of the *Shekhinah*, "I am a rose of Sharon a lily of the valleys" ([canticle 1-2][1] quoted from the *Zohar: The Book of Splendor*, selections ed.

by Scholem; Schocken, p. 118, i.e., "Song of Songs" [2:1-2]). To be sure, even as a reflection or image of the *Shekhinah*, Lili is never portrayed as an epitome of beauty and light too bright to be seen with human eyes on the Sabbath or any other time; she always appears as an ordinary figure in the novel; yet on Friday evenings at sunset, she appears the same and is still the *Shekhinah*, then as she is in the tenth *Sefirah* and in *"Lekha Dodi,"* the Sabbath song and prayer. As Ozick said in the Ciabattari interview, she had no wish or intention to write another novel about a survivor, but when Julian arrived in Paris, Lili was just there, and she could not help it; the character clearly evolved from that compulsion. Simply put, she is a survivor but an extraordinary one.

So is Lambert Strether, whose lust for life is reawakened only after he returns to Paris on a mission for his nominal fiancée to retrieve her son, Chadwick, from whatever attraction has kept him there. It is not, as he had believed, the lovely Mme. de Vionnet that holds Chad in Paris but Chad's own irresolution that has kept him there and is soon conquered; he is ready to leave for home, mother, and a prominent position in the family's immense company, his fortune virtually assured. Mme. de Vionnet and Paris are already for him the past; the family company and Woollett are his future, and soon after Strether leaves Paris behind, Chad will be on his way home, too. Strether, however, will not likely return to Woollett. Perhaps he will move out West, heed his own advice to Little Bilham, and live more fully than he had been doing since the death of his wife and child after which he had surrendered his independence to Mrs. Newsome and become only the editor's name imprinted on a green journal cover. No longer to be satisfied with a vacuous dependency, he leaves Paris ready to make a new start in mid-life.

In contrast to Strether's singular role as the protagonist and center-of-consciousness amid a multitude of active characters in James's *The Ambassadors*, Ozick's *Foreign Bodies* has a vastly wider setting that extends from Eastern Europe to Southern California with much time spent between them in Paris and New York City as well. In addition, elements of comic realism occur throughout the novel. For example, Marvin's coarse language in communicating especially with his son and sister, is often gross but hilarious although the matter is generally more serious than the language Marvin uses to discuss it. Happier and funnier are the references to Leo and Bea as a newly married couple attempting to enjoy their nights together sharing a minuscule one-room apartment with a huge grand piano—their wedding gift. Many of the scenes in *Foreign Bodies*, from early in the novel where the wedding of Bea's classmate is described with a vision of trained white doves flying over the heads of the guests; a celebration with dancing soon follows, which gives Leo the opportunity he had clearly anticipated to exhibit his fancy footwork as a dancer. Although dipping during the dance is familiar to Leo, it is not to Bea, who becomes dizzy for a moment and almost falls over backwards. After their own marriage sometime later, sans the festivity, the newlyweds try with dubious success to live and love in their one-room apartment with his grand piano towering over them. Moreover, the descriptions of the fraudulent Dr. Montalbano's sham but mostly successful medical practice are at times absurd, as is his difficulty as a Lothario attempting to seduce Iris, who has become his assistant; her desire and conscience appear to be at odds over the matter even while she lies stiff in the bed, evidently not as willing as she would like to be. Also, no less comic than pathetic is the experience of Beatrice during her surprise visit to Marvin's wife, Margaret, and discovering that the vile smell in her studio-room at the Suite Eyre Spa emanates from the somber painting on her easel, which had been rendered in excrement, probably her own.

Further, a mood of dark romanticism often prevails in scenes depicting the Marais, the Refugee Center, and other rundown places in Paris that reflect the dream-laden imagery of Bruno Schulz, whose imaginative, often grotesque prose was greatly admired by Cynthia Ozick since 1977, when *The Street of Crocodiles* was published by Penguin. It was Philip Roth, General Editor of "Writers from the Other Europe," the Penguin series in which it appeared, who brought Schulz's fiction to Ozick's attention, and in gratitude, she dedicated *The Messiah of Stockholm* to him the following year. At that time, she enthusiastically praised *The Street of Crocodiles* in a brief but rewarding essay, "The Phantasmagoria of Bruno Schulz," in *Art and Ardor* (1983), where she describes the slim volume as "a thick string of sights and sinuosities, a cascade of flashes, of extraordinary movements" (227). Schulz's second collection in English appeared as *Sanatorium under the Sign of the Hourglass* (Penguin 1979) two years after *The Street of Crocodiles;* it is a brilliant composition of related tales (see Kauver on Ozick and Roth, pp. 203-4, and 250n. 2).

Another motif in *Foreign Bodies* that becomes more evident and significant as the novel progresses is that of Jewish mysticism, including the concepts of *Tikkun*, "true marriage," and images of the *Shekhinah* as "the presence of God," which are implicit in much of the novel. It is a subtle theme but an increasingly meaningful one as the novel progresses, implicit in many references to Lili in particular throughout *Foreign Bodies*. Despite her poverty, her terrible war-wound, and her seeming frailty, Lili represents the figure of "great radiance called '*Shekhinah*'" in Jewish mysticism (Scholem, *Maj. Tr.*, 111). Her presence, behavior, and symbolic significance transform the novel from a chaotic family struggle into a mystical revelation that represents the act and function of *Tikkun*, the restoration of divine harmony in the world through benevolent action. *Tikkun* in *Foreign Bodies* enhances Ozick's narrative with brighter illumination and broader dimensions. Further, the mystical implications of Lili as a dark heroine "truly married" to the floundering Julian is crucial to him because, as he tells Iris, Lili is "the strongest person he'd ever known," "a small sturdy stem: you could bend it and it would arch and never break" (59). "She had taught him everything," he says, and is currently "teaching him the knowledge of death" (61, 129). Simultaneously she was subtly turning him toward Judaism. "I haven't got religion," he tell Iris; "I've got Lili" (59). Following such personal revelations and others from her younger brother, Iris realizes that he has changed and is gradually "becoming another Julian" (129). He has Lili to thank for drawing him back to the faith of his grandparents, whom she could not have known, as Strether in *The Ambassadors* must be grateful for heeding his own Jamesian advice after passing it on to a young countryman at a social gathering of elite aesthetes in Gloriani's garden as he prepares to leave Paris for the U.S. "Live, live, live fully while you can!" he urges little Bilham. Cynthia Ozick herself would have valued such Jamesian encouragement as a graduate student when she spent weeks and months in a library carrel writing her M.A. thesis, but for her the advice came years too late.

    According to Ozick a vigorous imagination is a more credible source of knowledge regarding the history of Jewish thought and faith than is Jewish mysticism. Yet she also said to Tom Teicholz in 1987: "The insight that the largest, deepest, widest imaginative faculty of all is what you need to be a monotheist teaches me that you simply cannot be a Jew if you repudiate the imagination" (Ozick in Teicholz, p. 168). Not less than a few moments before, she had stated, "Only a very strong imagination can rise to the idea of a non-corporeal God. . . . My hope is some day to be able to figure out a connection between the work of monotheism-imagining and the work of story-imagining. Until now I have thought of these as enemies" (p. 167).

But that "now" has passed. Guidelines provided by and developed in several excellent recent studies of Kabbalah clearly reveal that no enmity exists between them. As in the Bible these books testify to the historical affinity that exists between Kabbalah and the Holy Scriptures in terms of the media in which they are presented. For the many other scholars seeking a viable link among *Yahweh*, the Scriptures that testify to the existence of that sacred Being, and Kabbalah in order to perceive and recognize the imaginative pictorial affinity that relates them, many recent publications are readily available.

REFERENCES

Ciabattari, Jane. "Mad for Henry James," *Book Beast* (11/15/10); www. "Daily Beast," com.; includes a personal interview with Cynthia Ozick on Henry James and *Foreign Bodies*.

Cohen, Sarah Blacher. *Cynthia Ozick's Comic Art: From Levity to Liturgy*. Indianapolis: Indiana University Press, 1994.

James, Henry. *The Ambassadors, The Novels and Tales,* vols. 21-23. New York: Scribner's, 1909.

Kauvar, Elaine M. *Cynthia Ozick's Fiction: Tradition and Invention*. Bloomington: Indiana UP, 1993.

Kessner, Carole S. "*Foreign Bodies*: A Pentimento," *SAJL*, 31.2 (2012): 200-15.

Ozick, Cynthia. *Art & Ardor: Essays* (New York: Dutton, 1984); includes "The Fourth Sparrow: The Magisterial Reach of Gershom Scholem" (138-50), "The Lesson of the Master" (291-7), and "The Phantasmagoria of Bruno Schulz" (224-28).

"The Art of Fiction, XCV: Cynthia Ozick," interview by Tom Teicholz, *Paris Review* 29 (1987): 155-90.

___. *The Cannibal Galaxy*. New York: Knopf, 1983.

___. *Foreign Bodies*. Boston: Houghton Mifflin, 2010.

"Judging the World: Library of America's Bernard Malamud's Collections," *NYTBR* (3/16/14): 1ff.

____. *The Messiah of Stockholm*. New York: Knopf, 1987.

____. *The Puttermesser Papers*. New York: Knopf, 1997.

____. *The Shawl* [with *Rosa*]. New York: Knopf, 1989.

Pinsker, Sanford. "Lost Father, Lost Messiah," Review of *The Messiah of Stockholm*, by Cynthia Ozick, *Midstream* (Aug.-Sept. 1987): 59-60.

Scholem, Gershom S. *Major Trends in Jewish Mysticism*. New York: Schocken, 1961.

____. *On the Kabbalah and Its Symbolism*, trans. Ralph Manheim. New York: Schocken, 1965.

Teicholz, Tom. "Interview of Cynthia Ozick: The Art of Fiction," see above under Ozick.

Zohar: The Book of Splendor: Basic Readings from the Kabbalah. Ed. Gershom G. Scholem. New York: Schocken Books, 1949. Paperback ed., 1963.

4. Cynthia Ozick and the Christian Reader

Victor Strandberg

". . . identity is everything in life, isn't it?"—Trust (565)

The Christian reader in that title is me. I became Ozick's reader in the fall of 1981, after receiving a surprise letter from William Scheick, editor of *Texas Studies in Literature and Language*, requesting an essay for a special edition on three neglected American women writers: Anne Redmon, Shirley Hazzard, and Cynthia Ozick--the latter of whom was to be my subject. Having never heard of Ms. Ozick, I hurried to the stacks, read a couple of her books, and immediately realized that here was an extraordinarily gifted and original artist, a first rate talent beyond a doubt. The decision to accept the editor's proposal was easy.

In accepting Scheick's request, however, I felt obliged to correct a possible misunderstanding. Perhaps my name had led the editor to surmise that I am Jewish, and therefore competent to comprehend the Yiddish phrases that pepper Ozick's pages, to say nothing of the formidable array of Jewish scholars, artists, and rabbis she routinely cites along the way. In fact, I told him, my Swedish forebears bequeathed me an evangelical Christian heritage, making me fairly literate in Biblical lore but otherwise not qualified in Jewish Studies. So if the editor should prefer a seasoned Jewish scholar after all, there would be no protest on my part. No, I was told, I remained the editor's choice and should proceed.

As the first non-Jewish scholar to write substantially about Cynthia Ozick, I propose now, a third of a century later, to denote why a Christian reader like me takes an avid interest in so profoundly Jewish a writer. After rendering a comparison/contrast of our respective upbringings, featuring her interaction with the majority Christian culture and mine with the minority Jewish one (affected for both of us by our status as children of immigrants), I shall consider her use of Christian materials in her fiction (especially *Trust*), essays, and personal letters to me. Two crucial issues in this discourse will be how to define the concept of Jew and Christian, and how either heritage tries to cope with the overpowering force of evil we call the Holocaust—a dominant presence in Ozick's fiction and also in my moral (which for me means Christian) imagination.

1. Upbringings

"For better or worse, we are what we learned as children."
--Joan Didion

Growing up in the Christian (mostly Catholic) neighborhood of Pelham Bay, New York, Cynthia Ozick learned early on what she later called "fear of the goy." In Public School 71, she recalled,

I was the only Jewish kid . . . . There were two Catholic churches; I was terrified of them both, and was obliged to pass one or the other on the way to school; so, with shaking knees, I used to race past on the other side of the street. (Letter CO to VS, 6/6/90)

In later grades, she was ostracized for heresy: "in P.S. 71 I am publicly shamed in Assembly because I am caught not singing Christmas carols; in P.S. 71 I am repeatedly accused of deicide" (*Art & Ardor* [hereafter AA], 302). My earliest encounter with Judaism, by contrast, was entirely benign: a Sunday School lesson at age five about the Israelites murmuring against Moses. I recall asking what was bad about murmuring, and wondering, though not asking, what this story had to do with me.

My Christian education was delayed till age five because of my mother's mental illness, which sent her to an asylum and me to several foster homes. There I had no religious training whatever. During the first years of WWII, the public schools of Worcester County, Massachusetts made up for that oversight: I learned my first Christmas carol (Away in a Manger) in first grade, and I learned the Lord's Prayer as we all chanted it together every morning in our public elementary school. Such Jewish lore as I learned then and through my high school years came from the Bible study, sermons, and other discourse pertaining to our small working class congregation, which originally was Swedish-speaking but had to change to English so my generation could follow the services. In my congregation, no one ever accused the Jews of deicide. Instead, we understood that we ourselves were the guilty party, our sins having made Jesus' death on the Cross necessary. And one fundamental certainty, given our belief in the entire Bible as the infallible Word of God, was that the Israelites were/are God's Chosen People, divinely entitled to the land God promised them.

In her teens and early college years, Cynthia Ozick's main cultural dilemma was her sense of a contradiction between her Conservative Jewish heritage and her avid interest in pagan/Gentile (though not Christian) writings. After devouring *The Yellow Fairy Book* and Oscar Wilde's *Fairy Tales* in girlhood, she moved on to *The Aeneid, Jane Eyre*, Walter Scott, George Eliot, E. M. Forster and a wide assortment of secular works that threatened to woo her away from her Jewish matrix. Ozick's novella *The Pagan Rabbi* was her most brilliant rendering of this conflict, but it recurred frequently in other venues, most importantly, I think, through Tilbeck's role as a pagan demigod and Allegra's as an ardent Europhile in *Trust*. Going to secular and pagan sources for literary forebears enabled Ozick to sidestep the Christian dominance of her literary and cultural environment.

Until college, I was never aware of meeting anyone Jewish. In the ninth grade, the word "Yiddish" showed up in our reading, and only one classmate ventured a guess to its meaning. In the tenth grade, I supposed my typing teacher, Molly Shapiro, was Italian because of the final vowel in her name, and my Social Studies teacher with the comical name, Chester Garfunkel, said he was a Quaker. My education in contemporary Judaism, therefore, awaited the influence of a fellow freshman at Clark University named Joe Berman, whose Conservative practice paralleled that of my church. (My best friend in college, he also introduced me to my first hot pastrami sandwich.) Of course I met many other Jewish classmates at Clark University, but with little cultural impact. One oddity I noted about many of them was that I seemed to know their Hebrew Bible (then known to me as the Old Testament) better than they did—a huge advantage in my literary studies. But I had no doubt that the Christian Bible (then known to me as the New Testament) was the spiritually superior dispensation.

For a member of the majority culture, that conviction was easy to hold. As the first Christmas of my college years came near, it brought on a large, informal gathering of schoolmates lustily singing carols together. A note of discomfort first dawned on me when my devoutly observant friend Joe Berman remarked how "Even I," in his high school, sang carols with the others. By not singing carols with the others, Cynthia Ozick discovered something important about herself. In her cultural isolation, she learned that she could withstand the schoolyard bullying of the majority culture, fortified by the "mighty will" that Henry James considered the foremost need of the artist and consoled as well by the certainty of her intellectual superiority to her tormentors. But up the road a larger schoolyard awaited her arrival, in which her will would prove weak as a toothpick, her intellect a mote in the Zeitgeist's cold eye.

2. "Higher" Education

> *". . . majoring in Christianity and . . . the teaching of contempt"*
> –Cynthia Ozick

When Cynthia Ozick attended college, in the late forties and early fifties, the last fling of the WASP ascendancy was in its heyday. The iconic names of three Nobelists--Eliot, Faulkner, and Hemingway--dominated the literary scene, with the voices of Fitzgerald, Frost, Pound, and their like in the near background. For me, in the mid-fifties, the only problematic issue in this lineup was the expressly anti-Christian attitude of Wallace Stevens in "Sunday Morning" and elsewhere. For Cynthia Ozick, the problematics were more serious. The contemporary Fitzgerald revival, for example, pushed Gatsby's associate Meyer Wolfshiem into the foreground, flaunting his criminal "gonnegtions" and his cuff buttons made of human molars. And in 1948 the fanatical Jew-hater Ezra Pound was given the highest award America can give a poet, the Bollingen Prize.

William Faulkner, always his own man, appeared to differ from these compeers in portraying a highly intelligent and engaging "Semitic Man" in his second novel, *Mosquitoes* (1926). And in *The Sound and the Fury* (1929) he ridicules Jason Compson's battle against the "New York Jews" whom he blames for stealing his money on Wall Street. Yet, perhaps soured by his encounters with movie moguls during his sojourn in Hollywood, Faulkner spoke of the "jew owners of sweat shops" in his original Appendix to *The Sound and the Fury* in *The Portable Faulkner* (1946). Since this book was an attempt at a Faulkner revival (the plates for all but one of his books had been melted down for the war effort), Faulkner agreed to remove the phrase when his (Jewish) editor advised against raising the specter of anti-Semitism in a post-Holocaust environment.

Meanwhile, during postwar decades Hemingway's nasty portrait of Robert Cohn in *The Sun Also Rises* made not the slightest dent in either his popular appeal or his academic status as a giant of modern fiction. In real life, Cohn was based on Harold Loeb, a tennis partner and drinking buddy who helped Hemingway publish his first book, *In Our Time*. In the novel Cohn appears to embody a Philip Roth-like Goy-hunger, gazing at Lady Brett Ashley with an expression "a great deal as his compatriot must have looked when he saw the promised land." (Chapter III) But in real life, it was Hemingway who suffered unappeased erotic longing, and Cohn embodies Hemingway's act of revenge against Loeb for having bedded the prototype of Lady Brett Ashley (a woman named Duff Twysden), who had rejected Hemingway on the grounds that he was a married man. The petty jealousy aroused by this competition occasioned a remarkable intensity of malice, according to an ex-fiancee of Loeb's to whom Hemingway described his novel as follows: "I'm tearing those bastards apart. I'm putting everyone in it, and that kike Loeb is the villain." (Jeffrey Meyers, *Ernest Hemingway: A Biography,* 158)

But it was T. S. Eliot, the supreme literary deity of the age, who represented the epitome of anti-Jewish disdain. Early on, he created Jewish proprietors of notably low class brothels in "Sweeney Among the Nightingales" and "Burbank with a Baedeker, Bleistein with a Cigar." Somewhat later, "the jew" (small "j") "squats" (not "sits") on the window sill of his slumlord building in "Gerontion" (originally part of *The Waste Land*). Following his conversion in 1927, Eliot no longer ridiculed Jews for their lack of social grace. Now they posed the more serious danger of heresy. An ideal society, he told his audience at the University of Virginia, should be "homogenous," not "adulterated" by "foreign races," and therefore could not countenance the presence of too many "free-thinking Jews." (Peter Ackroyd, *T. S. Eliot: A Life*, 201) Unfree thinking was presumably OK. Or maybe free-thinking Gentiles.

Dismaying as they were, these sentiments were not the worst aspect of the Age of Eliot. Worse yet was the aura of papal infallibility that attended every pronouncement of the Great Man. Ozick herself describes that singular phenomenon as she had experienced it. In "T. S. Eliot at

101," she recalled his status as "a colossus, nothing less than a permanent luminary fixed in the firmament like the sun and the moon." Amazingly, for any poet, he did once "fill a football stadium. On April 30, 1956, fourteen thousand people came to hear him lecture on 'The Frontiers of Criticism' at the University of Minnesota." (FF, 6) The greatest names in contemporary criticism sang his praises, among whom she numbers William Empson, R. P. Blackmur, Hugh Kenner, F. R. Leavis, and F. O. Matthiessen.

It did not escape Cynthia Ozick's notice that Eliot, Hemingway, Fitzgerald and their anti-Semitic peers declared in various ways their Christian affinities. Following his conversion, T. S. Eliot was the most ardent of the lot, expressly devoting virtually everything he wrote to the propagation of "a Christian Society." For his part, Hemingway, though raised in the Congregational church, was deeply moved when given the last rites by a Catholic priest on the Italian front in 1918, and he converted officially to his second wife's Catholic faith when he married her in 1926. Fitzgerald, unlike Hemingway, was denied the last rites of the Church because the bishop of Baltimore considered him a bad Catholic, but his daughter Scottie eventually remedied that oversight by arranging a Catholic re-burial three decades later. Even Faulkner, the least orthodox of these writers, declared "I feel that I'm a good Christian" when asked about his religious status in an interview with college students. (*Faulkner in the University*, 203)

To a young Jewish woman raised by immigrant, working class parents and immersed in an academic climate of Eliot idolatry, the intimidation was complete. There was nothing to do but bow to the gods of the WASP ascendancy and accept the domination of a Christianized mode of literary study. As late as 1975, in her Preface to *Bloodshed*, she called *The Waste Land* "the greatest modern poem." Eventually, time and a change in the Zeitgeist made cultural independence attainable. In 1991, she deplored the "endemic anti-Semitism" in higher education, stating: "If you are an English major, you simply take it as your premise that you are majoring in Christianity and . . . as part and parcel of that in the teaching of contempt" ("The Changing Culture of the University," *Partisan Review* 58, no. 2, 1991 p.400) Now, in "T. S. Eliot at 101" (1989), she unmasks the master guru of her youth as "an autocratic, inhibited, depressed, rather narrow-minded and considerably bigoted fake Englishman." ("*Fame & Folly*, 7-8) Unfortunately, forty years earlier, in her formative years, such blasphemy was a dangerous commodity—thinkable, perhaps, but best left unexpressed.

As a Jew enduring a Christianized college culture, Ozick had plenty of company. I recall from my own graduate school years, a half-decade after hers, the incongruous spectacle of Jewish students and faculty alike probing earnestly into the mysteries of St John of the Cross and Dame Julian of Norwich so as to better understand Eliot's *Four Quartets*. Or scanning the Gospels so as to comprehend Faulkner's parade of Christ figures—Benjy in *The Sound and the Fury*, Joe Christmas in *Light in August*, Charles Bon in *Absalom, Absalom!*, the entire cast in *A Fable*. Or doing likewise to grasp the Passion Week allegory in Hemingway's *The Old Man and the Sea*. Or plumbing the Book of Revelation in homage to Steinbeck's *The Grapes of Wrath*. For me, such studies honored my religious heritage. For Cynthia Ozick, they seeded her own grapes of wrath, fermenting secretly, quietly until their time would come.

3. Trust: Return of the Repressed

"I was able to achieve, during its composition, wholesale revisions of self...."
--Letter, CO to VS, 1/14/82

That time did come round at last, ignited by the most apocalyptic event in her or my lifetime. About midway through her college years, after living "in the narrow throat of poetry," aesthetic bliss gave way to utter horror: "at last I am hammer-struck with the shock of Europe's skull, the bled planet of death camp and war" (MM 116). Most Americans, during those pre-television years, absorbed the Holocaust via the shocking photographs published by LIFE magazine soon after the war. In those same years, however, the onset of the Cold War made West Germany a crucial ally in that Manichean struggle between good and evil, and as the front line in that struggle, Germany became the site of a vast American investment—economic, political, and military. And so, as the Cold War intensified in the late forties and fifties, from the Berlin blockade of 1948 through the Korean War years, a prudent silence veiled the recent atrocities pertaining to both Germany and Japan. In addition, the unlimited American firebombing of civilians in enemy cities had muddied the ethical waters. American Jews, meanwhile, were largely absorbed in the rebirth of Israel, precariously placed among bitterly hostile neighbors and desperately in need of help. Response to the Holocaust would have to wait its turn.

For Cynthia Ozick, that turn came during the seven years she spent writing *Trust*, which she completed the day President Kennedy was murdered, November 22, 1963. "*Trust* went on and on for so many years," she says, "that I was able to achieve, during its composition, wholesale revisions of self, vast turnabouts of personality and character" (CO to VS letter, 1/14/82). Most notably, she changed from an American writer—by her own account, a would-be Henry James--into a Jewish one. Two events surely facilitated this metamorphosis: first, in 1960, the abduction from Argentina of Adolph Eichmann, the chief Nazi overlord of the Holocaust, who was tried and executed in Jerusalem; and second, the publication, in 1961, of a book by Raul Hilberg, the first and widely regarded as still the greatest of Holocaust historians. That book, *The Destruction of the European Jews* (abbreviated to *The Destruction*) comprises the protagonist's obsessive reading matter in "A Mercenary" (in *Bloodshed*), and its subject has affected Cynthia Ozick throughout her whole subsequent career. As *Trust* unfolded, the consciousness of the Holocaust increasingly pushed Jewish identity to dominance above all other themes.

The narrator's four parent figures in *Trust* represent this curve of rising intensity, with her mother, Allegra, and her biological father, Tilbeck, embodying the allure of Europe and the pagan enticement respectively. The narrator's other two parent figures (stepfathers) represent Christian and Jew, respectively. William, the Christian--a Calvinist Presbyterian—is a cold, dour, Puritanical figure whom the narrator never for one instant accepts as a father figure. Enoch Vand, the Jew, however, does overmaster the narrator's supposedly Gentile sensibility. Through him, the long-repressed matter of the Holocaust not only returns, it erupts with volcanic force: "it was deathcamp gas [that] . . . swarmed from his nostrils to touch those unshrouded tattooed carcasses . . . moving in freight cars over the gassed and blighted continent" (78). And though she tells her governess "I'm not Jewish" (67), her affinity with Enoch stamps in her consciousness a list of deathcamp names worthy of Raul Hilberg: "Dachau, Belsen, Auschwitz, Buchenwald, Maidenek, Chelmno, Treblinka, Mathausen, Sobibor" (76-78).

Given this history, it is not surprising that Ozick speaks of her "revulsion against the values—very plainly I mean the beliefs—of the surrounding culture. . . . It is a revulsion . . . against what is called, strangely, Western Civilization." (AA 157) That string of nouns—"values," "beliefs," "culture," "Civilization," all linked to "revulsion"—undeniably evoke a common adjective: "Christian." Ozick does not hesitate to make the connection. "Christianity does not stand responsible all alone in the world; nevertheless, it stands responsible," Ozick declares in "A Liberal's Auschwitz"—an essay that rebukes William Styron for highlighting the Gentile deaths in the eponymous deathcamp, thereby blurring its avowed purpose of murdering Jews. She proceeds to describe a long foreground of Christian complicity: "The Inquisition was the known fruit of concrete Christian power. The thirteenth-century Pope (his name was Innocent) who ordered Jews to wear the yellow badge was not innocent of its Nazi reissue seven hundred years later."

In *Trust*, Ozick prosecutes the case against Christianity mainly through her Gentile narrator. As a child she confused "the Holy Ghost with a new kind of candy bar" (59). As a young adult she speaks of "the bitter and loveless Christ" (38), and she condemns Christ's "cruelty in inventing and enforcing a policy of damnation" (375). She links God's indifference to the world's sufferings to the most widely propagated of all Christian Bible verses (John 3:16), with her own substitution for the word "Son": "God so loved the world that he gave his only begotten dung" (279). She changes the words of Jesus himself to comport with Holocaust consciousness, turning "In my Father's house are many mansions" (John 14:2) to "The house of death has many mansions" (80). She travesties a mainstream Protestant hymn, turning "Holy, Holy, Holy" into "wormy wormy wormy, early in the morning our curse shall rise to Thee" (66). Through Enoch she renders the judgment that "all Christians are heathen" (338), and "if she [Allegra] has no morals, she's a Christian" (338).

For the Christian reader, the main offense in these excerpts is their lack of psychological realism. It is unlikely that even a wholly disaffected ex-Christian would speak of a bitter and loveless Christ, confuse God's Son with dung, or downgrade the word *Holy* to *wormy*. By contrast, throughout *Trust* the case against Judaism is serious and credible, with Enoch Vand and his Gentile stepdaughter speaking alike of "God's cruelty" (279), of His non-existence ("Kein Gott ist," 136), and of His perverse mockery—turning Isaiah's Peaceable Kingdom, where the lion shall lie down with the lamb, into its Holocaust counterpart: "to have the murderer lie down with the murdered" (68-69). The case against the Jewish God culminates when Enoch calls Him "the

God of an unredeemed monstrosity . . . [and] worse worse worse, it's unredeemable" (397-8).

Ultimately, Ozick's theodicy extends to cosmic proportions: "Who can revere a universe which will take that lovely marvel, man (. . . aeons of fish straining toward the dry, gill into lung, paw into the dentist's and violinist's hand), and turn him into a carbon speck?" (373) (Perhaps if the universe could reply, it would point out that it also turned a carbon speck into man.) But waiting on the last page of *Trust* is Ozick's surprise resolution: she turns Enoch Vand from an atheistic font of despair into an Orthodox Jew. After reading the King James Bible all the way through, Enoch learns Hebrew so he can read the Bible again in its original language, then studies the Ethics of the Fathers, and "then he asked for the whole Talmud."

Whatever one thinks of this last-page conversion, it serves to bring Ozick's focus back to her central interest, not Holocaust-induced atheism and despair but Jewish identity. Belief might fluctuate at times as dramatized in "Bloodshed": "'Sometimes,' the rebbe said, 'even the rebbe does not believe. . . . It is characteristic of believers sometimes not to believe. And it is characteristic of unbelievers sometimes to believe.'" (*Bloodshed*, 72) Enoch Vand is Cynthia Ozick's surrogate in demonstrating this principle. Somewhere underneath his monstrous, ever-increasing load of Holocaust knowledge, Enoch Vand has retained his original identity: he is what he learned as a child. The Hebrew Bible, the Talmud, the Ethics of the Fathers: now he would re-learn them to reorient his bearings as an adult no longer protected by childhood innocence. Like Cynthia Ozick herself, he would somehow summon up the vast spiritual strength necessary to be, after the Holocaust, an observant Jew. Thus furnished, she could pursue her destined role as an artist.

4. A Common History

"I have [read] and will read any and any history of the Jews."
--Cynthia Ozick (Letter 1/14/82)

"After *Trust* I became a Jewish writer," Ozick has said. (Letter 10/26/82) In her review/rebuke of John Updike's *Bech: A Book*, she clarifies that statement by indicating who is *not* a Jewish writer. Certainly not Bech, Updike's version of a Jewish writer assembled "out of Mailer,

Bellow, Singer, Malamud, Fuchs, Salinger, [and] the two Roths." Both Bech and his real life models, she explains, lack two essential features. First, as "disaffected, de-Judaized Jewish novelists of his generation," they "miss the deepest point of all": "Being a Jew is something more than being an alienated marginal sensibility with kinky hair. Simply: to be a Jew is to be covenanted; or, . . . at the very minimum, to be aware of the Covenant itself." (AA 117, 122-3) The other missing feature is best described in Ozick's review of Mark Harris's *The Goy*, about a Gentile who wants to become a Jew. "What is the Jewish 'secret?'" she writes. "What makes a Jew is the conscious implication in millennia. To be a Jew is to be every moment in history, to keep history for breath and daily bread." ("Jews and Gentiles," *Commentary*, June 1971, 106)

For a taste of that bread, a passage from "Levitation" can stand in for many similar episodes. First, Ozick observes a perilous incompatibility between Jewish husband and Gentile wife: "Volumes of Jewish history ran up and down their walls; they belonged to Feingold. Lucy read only one book—it was *Emma*—over and over again" (*Levitation*, 6-7). Then those histories yield up their catch:

"Feingold wanted to talk about . . . certain historical atrocities, abominations: to wit, the crime of the French nobleman Draconet, a proud Crusader, who in the spring of the year 1247 arrested all the Jews of the province of Vienne, castrated the men, and tore off the breasts of the women. . . . It interested Feingold that the Magna Carta and the Jewish badge of shame were issued in the same year. . . . How in London, in 1279, Jews were torn to pieces by horses, on a charge of having crucified a Christian child. How 1285, in Munich, a mob burned down a synagogue on the same pretext. . . . Feingold was crazed by these tales, he drank them like a vampire." (*Levitation*, 11-12)

To be a Jew, Ozick says, is to assimilate such stories. For that reason the goy in Mark Harris's *The Goy* cannot become a Jew: because "fear of the goy" has become part of Jewish identity.

Fear of the goy was, for Ozick, a family inheritance. In Czarist Russia, her own father was nearly incinerated at age five when a mob egged on by a priest drove the Jews of the village into their synagogue and prepared to burn it. The chance intervention of a good priest dissolved the mob and saved those lives. On her mother's side, a great-uncle and his son were dragged by horses over cobblestones until their skulls shattered. In an essay called "The Modern Hep Hep Hep" Ozick cites her favorite historian, Heinrich Graetz, to verify gruesome episodes spanning millennia of Jewish life:

"If Jewish history were to follow chronicles, memorial books and martyrologies, its pages would be filled with bloodshed, it would consist of horrible exhibitions of corpses. . . . There were Geman Christian families who boasted that they had burnt Jews, and in their pride assumed the name of *Judenbrater* (Jew-roaster)."

This is Jewish history, but not only Jewish history. It also belongs to the history of Christianity. We could likewise describe it as European history and World history, but what matters for Jews and Christians is that it is our common history. I did not have relatives who were incinerated in Auschwitz, nor, as far as I know, were any of my ancestors burned alive for drinking Christian blood. But I have ingested the horror. Like Feingold in "Levitation," I too am "crazed by these tales." I too "[drink] them like a vampire." Like Cynthia Ozick, I am particularly fixated on the Holocaust, because it happened during my lifetime in what was conventionally thought to be the most civilized area of the earth. I have traveled to Dachau, Auschwitz, and the Anne Frank House. And I have studied Holocaust history.

To illustrate this history-hunger, I will select from my readings and other sources three ghoulish episodes (not the worst) that have become my familiar mental companions. First, a survivor's tale how, circa 1942, a vehicle passed down his street with a loudspeaker ordering all Jews to report to the field next the train station at a certain hour. When he, a small boy, arrived with his parents he saw two SS men grabbing each baby from arriving families and heaving them into a nearby pile. Second is the face of a specific Sonderkommando in *The Auschwitz Album* (photos taken by an SS man). The Sonderkommandos were Jewish inmates who were compelled to process the incoming trainloads of new victims, herding them to their deaths in the gas chambers and cleaning up the mess inside the railcars that transported them. I think of that specific Sonderkommando, of the expression on his face, in connection with the third of these episodes, described by another Sonderkommando who recalled his experience in a "fiction" titled "This Way to the Gas, Ladies and Gentleman." I stand alongside this man as the message is passed around, "A transport is coming." I share his stare as "the train rolls slowly along the ramp. In the tiny barred windows appear pale, wilted, exhausted human faces, terror-stricken women with tangled hair, unshaven men."

In my mind I keep seeing those faces, and I see also the SS man who approaches the emptied railcar, puts his head in, recoils from the stench, and orders the Sonderkommando to clean it up. With him I enter the car: "In the corner amid human excrement. . . lie squashed, trampled infants, naked little monsters with enormous heads and bloated bellies. We carry them out like chickens, holding several in each hand."

    The author of this "story," Tadeusz Borowski, committed suicide at age 29. I think I know why. For him and many other survivor suicides, the cause was not survivor's guilt—or not only survivor's guilt. I m, t was knowing too much. The Book says no man can see God and live; its corollary is that no man can see too much depravity and live, either. Even if the body lives on, the soul dies. The photographed expression on that Sonderkommando's face is, for me, one verification of this insight. Another verification comes via the great historian Raul Hilberg, who lived to age 81 but whose soul, it appears, fared less enviably. In the last paragraph of his memoir *The Politics of Memory*, Hilberg cites a letter sent to him by someone he never knew, a survivor named H. G. Adler. Responding to his reading of *The Destruction*, Adler made Hilberg feel "as though he [Adler] had peered directly into the core of my being." And this, in the book's final sentence, is what Adler found: "At the end, nothing remains but despair and doubt about everything, because for Hilberg there is only recognition, perhaps a grasp, but certainly no understanding." Unlike Enoch Vand, Hilberg became, during his lifelong immersion in Holocaust research, an atheist. To be a Jew is to be every moment in history, perhaps, but for Hilberg too much Jewish history snuffed out the other central feature of Jewish identity, the Covenant.

    The obvious question, then, is why do I study this soul-crushing matter—the Holocaust, mainly, but also books about the depravities of Stalin, Lenin, Mao, and their henchmen. The reason is that these works speak truth, though not the whole truth, about our human species. The whole truth comprehends not only the mystery of iniquity but also its opposite counterpart, the inexplicable mystery of goodness—the latter often occurring in response to the former. My several visits to the Holocaust Museum in Washington have disclosed just such a profile. A visitor to the Museum takes an elevator to the top floor and then walks down a long ramp through displays of unspeakable evil featuring both perpetrators and victims--photographs, film clips, an actual railcar used for transport, and perhaps most appalling of all, huge piles of sheared off human hair and vacant shoes. It is scarcely credible that humankind is capable of such monstrous wickedness on so vast a scale.

It surprised me, and probably many others, to find that this immersion in evil does not extend to the end of the tour. Instead, the final room the Museum visitor will enter renders a tribute to extra-ordinary goodness. From a letter I sent Ms. Ozick in December, 2004, the following excerpt will serve to explain my reaction to this arrangement, probably shared by many others:

About the Museum, I hope you won't think it perverse that, as much as anything else, the gallery of Righteous Gentiles moves me to tears every time. Not because I am one, but because these individuals, unlike the other victims, had a choice. All they had to do to go on living is shut up and mind their own business, and they refused to do it. The conscience of these people, some of them just teenagers, is like an eternal flame against the dark—it is really and truly eternal, if anything is.

Cynthia Ozick expressed similar sentiments in an essay titled "On Christian Heroism." Here she describes the Yad Vashem building in Jerusalem as not only a memorial to victims of Holocaust horror but also "a grove of celebration and honor: a grand row of trees, one for each savior, marks the valor of the Christian rescuers of Europe, the Righteous Among the Nations." It is significant that her title applies the word "Christian" to people who may not have thought of themselves as Christian in any fashion--

those extraordinary souls who refused to stand by as their neighbors were being hauled away to the killing sites. . . . They are the heroes of Nazified Europe. They are Polish, Italian, Romanian, Russian, Hungarian, French, Yugoslavian, Swiss, Swedish, Dutch, Spanish, German. They are Catholic and Protestant. They are urban and rural; educated and uneducated; sophisticated and simple; they include nuns and socialists. And whatever they did, they did at the risk of their lives. (FF 203-4)

In calling all these folk Christians, Ozick echoes, wittingly or not, the words of Jesus, who, when asked to distinguish his true followers from others, said "By their fruits you shall know them." Cynthia Ozick and her Christian reader agree absolutely on this point: behavior defines the category. My favorite confirmation of this principle occurs in Matthew 25:35, where Jesus divides his true followers from the false--the sheep from the goats: "For I was hungry and you gave me meat; I was thirsty and you gave me drink; I was a stranger and you took me in." (Think what that last phrase means vis-à-vis Ozick's "Christian" heroes of the Holocaust). When some of his "sheep" protest that they never gave Jesus any such thing, he agrees, but declares that when they gave to "the least of these"—the neediest—that was the same as giving to him. And vice-versa for the "goats," those whom Jesus repudiates for failing to do for the neediest even though they had given Jesus himself what he listed. Jesus says no word here about baptism, the Creed, the Sacraments: only behavior matters.

"You are the light of the world," Jesus went on to say about his true followers. Ozick ends "On Christian Heroism" with a similar encomium:

. . . those who undertook the risks, those who bravery steeped them in perilous contingencies, those whose moral strength urged them into heart-stopping responsibility. . . . These few are more substantial than the multitudes from whom they distinguished themselves; and it is from these undeniably heroic and principled few that we can learn the full resonance of civilization. (FF 207)

5. A Common Ethos

"Who is their God?" –Martin Luther King, Jr.

"I want to be known!" Cynthia Ozick exclaimed regarding her religious heritage— "I want my neighbors to assimilate my perceptions as I have assimilated theirs; I want them to know the real Hannukkah of history. . . . I want them to know the real Passover, the real Rosh ha-Shanah and Yom Kippur, as I know Allhallows Eve and Whitsundtide and Easter and Saint Francis. . . ." ("A Liberal's Auschwitz"). In the deepest sense, we can't be known, because of what we did not learn as children. She did not sing Christmas carols or chant the Lord's Prayer, and I did not have a clue about Yom Kippur. But given our agreement about the proper definition of "Christian"—as a category defined by behavior-- perhaps we can extend our mutual understanding.

In her twenties, Cynthia Ozick read an essay by the eminent rabbi Leo Baeck entitled "Romantic Religion" which, she says, "broke open the conceptual egg of my life." (Letter, 1/14/82) Here Baeck drew a sharp contrast between the Jewish "Classical" or Rational religion and its Romantic (implicitly Christian) counterpart. Romantic religion inhabits "the realm . . . which lies beyond all reality. . . . Romantic religion is completely opposed to the whole sphere of existence with which the social conscience is concerned. . . . Romanticism therefore lacks any strong ethical impulse, any will to conquer life ethically." In her own voice Ozick added the precept that "in rabbinic Judaism (which *is* Judaism) there aren't any miracles or bizarre contrary-to-nature beliefs, . . . inquiry is encouraged, . . . rationalism rules." (Letter, 8/11/90) Striving toward ultimate conciseness, she calls Judaism "ethical monotheism."

Complicating this analysis is her notation that the Romantic/Rationalist divide signifies "an inherent split in the human psyche" between "those that thrive on mysticism (immanence, incarnation) and those that thrive on rationalism." This split "occurs within Judaism, Christianity, Islam. . . [and] sometimes in the same mind!" (Letter, 7/20/91)Here is another opportunity for Ozick and her Christian reader to find common ground. On closer view, both Judaism and its Christian offspring encompass Rational and "Romantic" features. The foundational stories of Judaism do include miracles and contrary-to-nature beliefs—the sun standing still on behalf of an Israelite army; Moses conversing with a Burning Bush and parting the waters of the sea; Elijah traveling skyward in a supernatural chariot. Conversely, the Christian Gospels do include, along with their miracles, a compelling ethical power.

To honor that ethical impulse in both Jewish and Christian practice, it is necessary to place each tradition under scrutiny, a process that requires independent thinking. So considered, the proper use of tradition is to transmit information, not to compel obedience. Every generation in its turn is called upon to weed the garden of Sacred Writ, to prune the tree of Righteousness. Otherwise the Divine Will would still be understood to condone slavery, malice toward lepers, the abject oppression of women, the killing of witches and homosexuals, and the imposition of inherited guilt. Even the hallowed Decalogue requires precisely this sort of winnowing, most clearly regarding the same Second Commandment which, as it happens, Cynthia Ozick considers theologically definitive for Jewish identity: "a Jew is someone who shuns idols. . . . The Commandment against idols is above all a Commandment against victimization and in behalf of pity." (AA, 188, 190) But the Second

Commandment includes language that denies pity, thereby summoning forth Stephen Crane's fierce rebuke in the name of pity (in "The Sins of the Fathers"):

> "And the sins of the fathers shall be
> visited upon the heads of the children,
> even unto the third and fourth
> generation of them that hate me."
>
> Well, then I hate thee, unrighteous picture;
> Wicked image, I hate thee;
> So, strike with thy vengeance
> The heads of those little men
> Who come blindly.

The Christian tradition also requires pruning, as its long history of persecuting Jews makes appallingly clear. For Protestant Christians, this process occurs under the defining principle of the Protestant heritage, freedom of conscience. Inevitably, this principle has bred a broad patchwork of denominations ranging from the questionably Christian Unitarians on the left to the hardshell fundamentalists on the right, espousing vastly various systems of belief and codes of behavior. Among American writers, three familiar names bear witness to that broad spectrum. At one extreme is T. S. Eliot's ultra-orthodox tradition, in whose name he declared "the whole of modern literature" to be "corrupted" by its denial of "the primacy of the supernatural over the natural life." ("Religion and Literature"). As an engaging example of this belief, he once stated an intention to write an essay on the devil in modern literature--not portrayals of the devil, but the presence of the devil. It is disappointing to learn, in Lyndall Gordon's *Eliot's New Life*, that Eliot's religious motive was fear. In 1919, eight years before his conversion, he told Ezra Pound "I am afraid of the life after death." (*New Life*, 37) Even after his conversion, he told another friend that he walked in daily terror of damnation. (34)

At the opposite extreme, Robert Penn Warren embraced what appears to be Christian atheism: "I think a man just dies. No heaven. No hell. . . . I'm a naturalist. I don't believe in God. . . . But. . . what I want to try to emulate now, is the example of Jesus. . . . I want to give myself in sacrifice of some sort."(Joseph Blotner's *Robert Penn Warren*, 450) And somewhere between Eliot and Warren is William Faulkner, telling his interviewer Jean Stein that ""everyone is a Christian, depending on your definition of the word," which he went on to define as "trying to be a little better than nature made you." Queried about his beliefs in Japan, in 1955, Faulkner declared "I believe in God," but he was not so sure about Christian practice : "Sometimes Christianity gets pretty debased. . . . but I believe that man has a soul that aspires to what we call God. . . . The trouble with Christianity is that we have never tried it yet." In Faulkner's South, he had seen much evidence to support this judgment.

From the foregoing variety of perspectives, we may infer the first principle of Christian practice: I, the practitioner, decide what it entails. Not the Pope, not Billy Graham, nor any other exponent of high religious authority. This freedom of conscience offers the prospect of more common ground between the Jewish writer and her Christian reader. In her interview with Elaine Kauvar, Cynthia Ozick discloses how far she has moved in this direction. Whereas she had once implicated Christianity in the Holocaust, thereby fueling her hatred of Western/Christian civilization, she now describes "Judaism in its ontological and moral aspects" as a heritage that "all of Western civilization shares." More specifically, "you just can't have a Christian culture without understanding that it is also a Jewish culture." Exactly so, says her Christian reader: Christian identity has a Jewish base.

To begin, we must acknowledge that Jesus of Nazareth was not a Christian. He was, and considered himself, quintessentially a Jew. Throughout the Gospels he binds himself with ropes of steel to the only sacred writ he knew, the Hebrew Bible. No tag line in the Gospels is more repetitious than "all this was done so that which was written might be fulfilled." His discourse is studded with Biblical citations—to the Decalogue, to the Book of Jonah, to the prophet Isaiah, to Jeremiah, to the Psalms. The first page of the first Gospel (Matthew) traces Jesus' lineage through every Jewish generation back to Abraham, pointedly including David and Solomon as direct ancestors. And until the priesthood rejected his ministry, he aimed his mission exclusively at his people Israel, so much so as to sometimes exhibit what might later be called unChristian behavior. When a Gentile "woman of Canaan" asks him to heal her daughter, for example, he answers "I am not sent but unto . . . the house of Israel," and when she persists he compares her to a dog: "It is not meet to take the children's bread, and to cast it to dogs." That her reply, "Truth, Lord: yet the dogs eat of the crumbs which fall from their master's table," causes him to relent and heal the girl does not absolve his gratuitous insult. (Matthew 15: 22-28)

Most crucially, the source of Jesus' obsession with the poor and needy is Hebrew scripture. It traces back to the first generation after Adam's Fall, when his son Cain directs sarcasm at his Maker: "Am I my brother's keeper?" Though God chooses not to answer that rhetorical question, His answer is threaded throughout the rest of the Hebrew Bible: in Job's claim to righteousness (29:12): "I delivered the poor that cried, and the fatherless, and him that had none to help him"; in Psalm 82, where God threatens to bust his subordinate gods down to mere human status for their failure to "Defend the poor and fatherless. . . [to] Deliver the poor and needy"; and in the thunderous words of Jesus' greatest predecessor, the prophet Isaiah (whom Jesus quotes more than any other source): "the spoil of the poor is in your houses. What mean ye that ye. . . grind the faces of the poor? saith the Lord" (Isaiah 3: 14-15).

Jesus apparently inherited his campaign against the priesthood from his great predecessor as well. His eightfold repetition in Matthew 23-- "Woe unto you, scribes and Pharisees, hypocrites!"—bears the stamp of Isaiah's opening chapter: "To what purpose is your multitude of sacrifices unto me? Saith the Lord. . . . Bring no more vain oblations; incense is an abomination to me; the new moons and Sabbaths, the calling of assemblies, I cannot away with; it is iniquity" (I: 13-14). Most consequentially, to world history at large, Jesus inherited the Messianic prophecies from Isaiah 9, 11 and 53—the basis of the Christian orthodoxy. Even Jesus' command to forgive one's enemies may be rooted in Isaiah 19:24-25: "In that day shall Israel be the third with Egypt and with Assyria. . . Whom the Lord of hosts shall bless, saying, Blessed be Egypt my people, and Assyria the work of my hands, and Israel mine inheritance."

Unfortunately, Isaiah also bequeathed some noxious weeds to his Christian successors, among them a tradition of misogyny. When Jesus saved an adulteress from being stoned with his famous line, "Let him without sin cast the first stone," he declined to remark that her adulterous lover was nowhere in view. So, too, when Isaiah denounces the young women of Israel for their sexual turpitude in chapter 3, he declares that God will "smite with a scab the crown of the head of the daughters of Zion" but says nothing about their sex partners (who left them pregnant and unmarried in chapter 4). The tradition of an all male priesthood and exclusion of women from the minyan also represent weeds of unconscionable longevity in the sacred garden.

So far as Christian scripture is concerned, the most noxious weed that needs uprooting is obviously the concept of hell—a murky idea in the Bible that was all too vividly clarified by later theologians. The prospect of suffering unbearable torture throughout eternity, which has terrorized countless millions into adopting the faith (apparently including T. S. Eliot), is an unworthy motive for Christian worship. Whether or not this concept is valid—that is, whether hell really exists—is irrelevant to the Christian reader's response, which revises Cynthia Ozick's definition of a Jew by a single word. Whereas Ozick says "a Jew is someone who shuns idols," her reader—in the name of freedom of conscience--says "a Christian is someone who shuns cruelty." The Christian reader condemns the concept of hell as the cruelest idea ever conceived by anyone, a monstrosity incompatible with the Christian conscience.

To shun cruelty is to thwart the perversion of conscience which condones evil behavior and calls it good. The world wide prevalence of that perversion is why shunning cruelty is the most crucial feature of a valid Christian conscience. It overrides many segments of the Book in which cruelty is celebrated—not just the prospect of Hell but also the Tribulation and the Rapture in the Christian Bible, along with the various massacres of enemy civilians in the Hebrew Bible. (Perhaps the most egregious of these relates to the Passover, in which all Egyptian families lose their first-born children, as though Pharoah had asked their opinion about letting God's people go.)

The Bible stands supreme in sacred literature. No portrayal of God that I know of appeals so much as His personality in the Book of Jonah, gently reproving instead of annihilating the disobedient servant. (Jonah is appealing too—a remarkably courageous fellow in his turn.) Anyone who wants moral guidance will find no better statement anywhere than the last sentence of this Book, where God will not annihilate Israel's deadliest enemy because Ninevah contains 120,000 children "who do not know their right hand from their left," and—what I find stunning—"also much cattle." The world's conscience has not yet caught up with these words. You don't have to be a vegetarian to be horrified at the way the hogs, cattle, chickens, veal calves, and their like pass their wretched lives in the factory farms we depend on. How admirable it is that the Book of Jonah is recited in its entirety every year on the highest holy day on the Jewish calendar, Yom Kippur. How excellent too that the Christian Bible includes all of Hebrew scripture, thus bringing Jonah's God to the Gentiles.

6. Aspirations

> *". . . the deepest human life is everywhere, is eternal."*
> –William James, in "What Makes a Life Significant"

At its strongest, religion is more than a system of ethics; it also envisions a metaphysical dimension that governs the individual's relationship to eternity. Probably the greatest attraction of Christianity for two millennia has been its appeal on this level, extending to its followers the promise of eternal life in the kingdom of God. Concerning this and other metaphysical doctrines, including the status of Jesus as Messiah, Son of God, and Incarnation of God, the Christian reader defers judgment, not because these doctrines are unimportant or invalid but because he lacks the wisdom to understand such conceptions. In this regard, Herman Melville offers a model to live by. As Ishmael leaves Father Mapple's chapel, he observes the good pastor kneeling to offer a prayer: "I leave eternity to Thee, for what is man that he should live out the lifetime of his God?" Genuine piety does not require a reward in the next world. And so far as this life is concerned, the only reward goodness craves is significance, the sense that sacrifice matters.

Because nature gives no proof that goodness matters—in fact, gives much disheartening proof to the contrary—belief in goodness must be taken on faith, a metaphysical proposition. So here is where ethics and metaphysics meet, in the conviction that goodness may have permanent meaning. Although much commentary throughout the Bible supports that conviction, its most persuasive formulation is found, I think, elsewhere, in the writings of William James. Two excerpts will make the case. The first, from the essay "Pragmatism and Religion," assigns an ultimate meaning to ethical action:

"I believe that each man is responsible for making the universe better and that if he does not do this it will be in so far left undone. . . . Suppose the world's author put the case to you before creation, saying: 'I am going to make a world not certain to be saved, a world the perfection shall be conditional merely, the condition being that each several agent does its own level best. I offer you the chance of taking part in such a world. Its safety, you see, is unwarranted. It is a real adventure, with real danger. . . .'"

This notion that God's work is our own comports well with Cynthia Ozick's view that our divinely imposed ethical obligation is the *only* thing we can know about God: ". . . what God *is* (the whole kit and caboodle of mysticism) is not our human business. *Our* business is to go about trying to make an ethical civilization" (Letter 8/11/90).

To step beyond ethics into metaphysics—contemplation of God-- entails, for Ozick, a grave risk of idolatry. Thus, in *Trust*, Enoch Vand regards God as "a principle which it is blasphemy to visualize" (375). In her own voice she says, "We can't presume to give a face or a name or a shape to the Creator, or set any limits of our own, or presume to define or imagine qualities or attributes" (Letter 8/11/90). The problem with this version of the Second Commandment is that the ordinance is unobeyable. Anyone who maintains a belief in God cannot suppress the impulse to imagine what that Deity is like, at least in a tentative fashion. Our final excerpt from William James, therefore, represents agreement between Cynthia Ozick and her Christian reader so far as its ethical content is concerned, but a difference of opinion regarding its visual imagery. Drawn from *The Varieties of Religious Experience*, the excerpt describes a woman's vision of lives being used by a Higher Power to attain an unknowable ultimate purpose:

"A great Being or Power was traveling through the sky, his foot was on a kind of lightning asa wheel is on a rail, it was his pathway. The lightning was made entirely of the spirits of innumerable people close to one another, and I was one of them. He moved in a straight line, and each part of the streak or flash came into its short conscious existence only that he might travel. I seemed to be directly under the foot of God. . . . I was the means of his achieving and revealing something, I know not what or to whom. . . ." (pp. 301-302)

Anyone whose life has moved that Being or Power a billionth of an inch across the sky has had a meaningful existence. But a life cannot attain permanent significance on its own. Significance requires interaction with other lives in a specific context of time, place, and circumstance. Such interaction, in the context of our Western tradition , can aspire to the creation of a Christian society. Which is to say, a Judaic society—as even T. S. Eliot finally came around to acknowledge. In a furious rebuke to Ezra Pound, Eliot declared that he would accept Pound's ridicule of himself but he would not tolerate any ridicule of his religion, which he defined as the Jewish religion. (Because of copyright issues, Lyndall Gordon could not quote Eliot's letter directly, but she described the incident indirectly as follows: "After 1936, Eliot resisted the continued virulence of Pound's anti-Semitism, and on 13 August 1954 let fly one furious rebuff to the effect that, although Pound was at liberty to continue with personal insults, Eliot would tolerate no further insult either to his nationality or to his religion, which was the Jewish religion." [*Eliot's New Life*, Farrar, Straus and Giroux, New York, 1988, p. 341].)

The logic seems binding: If Jesus declared himself a Jew, and if his acolyte Eliot, two millennia later, claimed adherence to the Jewish religion, can Cynthia Ozick's Christian reader do otherwise? Much depends on how we define "the Jewish religion." In an irremediably profound way, Ozick's definition, absorbed from her lifelong experience and study, must differ from Eliot's or mine. Then again, it also differs from that of other Jews, including members of her own congregation. So, too, my own Christian belief differs not only from that of most believers but from the sayings of Jesus himself. I not only reject his exclusivity ("no man comes to the Father but by me"—John 14:6) but I do so in favor of a doctrine found nowhere in either the Christian or Hebrew Bible, namely that cruelty is the one unforgiveable sin. I reject the former doctrine as incompatible with the latter one.

In the name of freedom of conscience, then, the Christian reader forsakes the exclusivity of his religious heritage. But the Jewish heritage also has an exclusivity issue: an overly Orthodox ethos proposes limitations based on tribal identity. On the other hand, given the tenacity of these doctrines, for two thousand years in one instance and twice that for the other, perhaps a split-level consciousness is the final answer. Let Christians and Jews maintain their respective exclusivities at one level of their thinking while keeping that level ultimately subordinate to a larger enterprise—the entire human project.

Within that project, Christians and Jews occupy a distinguished place thanks to their mutual debt. To Judaism, Christianity owes its claim to the Holy Writ of ancient Israel as the portal to a meaningful life and a humane society. But Judaism also owes a debt to its Christian offspring. By historical happenstance (the spread of the great Western empires), the Christian Bible, which includes the Hebrew Bible, has extended the Judaic ethic across two thousand years and six continents to encompass Cynthia Ozick and her Christian reader in a common matrix of cultural identity. Within that matrix indelible differences persist which merit respect in both directions. For the Christian reader, those differences enrich the writings of Cynthia Ozick, infusing our common heritage with deeper interest.

REFERENCES for CYNTHIA OZICK AND THE CHRISTIAN READER

I. Writings by Cynthia Ozick

Trust. New York: New American Library, 1966.
The Pagan Rabbi and Other Stories. New York: Knopf, 1971.
Bloodshed and Three Novellas. New York: Knopf, 1976.
Levitation: Five Fictions. New York: Knopf, 1982.
Art & Ardor. New York: Knopf, 1983.
Metaphor & Memory. New York: Knopf, 1989.
Fame & Folly. New York: Vintage Books, 1996.
"The Changing Culture of the University," *Partisan Review* 58 no. 2, 1991, 400.
"A Liberal's Auschwitz," *The Pushcart Prize: First Edition* (New York: 1976-77), 152.
"Jews and Gentiles," *Commentary*, June, 1971, 106.
Letters, Cynthia Ozick to/from Victor Strandberg

II. Other Sources

Joan Didion, "On Morality," in *Slouching Toward Bethlehem* (New York: Delta Books, 1968), 158.

Ernest Hemingway, *The Sun Also Rises* (Chapter III, any edition).

Jeffrey Meyers, *Ernest Hemingway: A Biography*. New York: Harper and Row, 1985, 158.

Peter Ackroyd, *T. S. Eliot: A Life*. New York: Simon and Schuster, 1984, 201.

Lyndall Gordon, *Eliot's New Life*. New York: The Noonday Press, (FSG), 1988, 34, 37, 341.

Frederick Gwynn and Joseph Blotner, *Faulkner in the University*. New York, Vintage Books, 1965, 203.

Tadeusz Borowski, "This Way to the Gas, Ladies and Gentlemen."

Raul Hilberg, *The Politics of Memory*. Chicago: Ivan R. Dee, 1996.

Joseph Blotner, *Robert Penn Warren: A Biography*. New York: Random House, 1997, 450

Jean Stein, Interview with William Faulkner. *The Paris Review Interviews*, New York: 1959, 132.

Elaine Kauvar, Interview with Cynthia Ozick, *Contemporary Literature* 26, no. 4 (Winter 1985)

William James, *The Varieties of Religious Experience*. (New York: Mentor Books, 1968), 275, 301-2

William James, *Pragmatism* (New York: New American Library, 1955), 175, 181.

William James, "What Makes a Life Significant." *Talks to Teachers. . .* , New York: 1929, 274-278, 299.

5. Cynthia Ozick's Classical Feminism

Daniel Walden

Feminism means many things to many people before THE 1960S and 1970s, feminist ideology took little cognizance of women's self-identification besides gender. True, women's rights advocates in the nineteenth and early twentieth centuries struggled for individual autonomy and access to all those prerogatives men had and took for granted – access to higher education, being employed, the law, medicine, and the ballot. On the one hand, women claimed they were equal to men in everything and, therefore, deserved the same or equal opportunities as men enjoyed. On the other hand, as Nancy Cott explains, women pointed out that their sex, their biology, differed from the male, that females as a result were more moral, nurturing, and pacific, while males were competitive, aggrandizing, physical, belligerent, and self-interested (Cott 1986, 490-91). In Cynthia Ozick's view, as a fiction writer, she rejects the phrase "woman writer" as antifeminist. As she put it in a 1977 *Atlantic Online* interview: in the 1970s, at the height of the "neo-feminist movement," "[i]t was becoming apparent that there were going to be two categories of writers – writers and women writers" (1997, 2). In fact, this has nearly come about, as she stated in the same interview: "People often ask how I can reject the phrase 'woman writer' and not reject the phrase 'Jewish writer' – a preposterous question. 'Jewish' is a category of civilization, culture, and intellect, and 'woman' is a category of anatomy and physiology. It's rough thinking to compare vast cultural and intellectual movements with the capacity to bear children" (Ozick 1977). In short, Cynthia Ozick is a classical feminist.

In her 1965 book, *The Ideas of the Woman Suffrage Movement 1890-1920*, Aileen Kraditor argued that these approaches in the American suffrage movement might be dubbed the natural rights or "justice" argument and the others argued from "expediency." In reminiscences of women born in the 1850s to the 1880s, one can find the genesis of these views in uncomplicated rage at male dominance, the arbitrariness of male privilege, and jealousy of male prerogatives, even when – perhaps because – one finds affirmation of female character (Kraditor 1965, 37-43, 87-91). Perhaps Harriet Burton Laidlaw caught the tenor of the message best in her 1912 opinion that insofar as women were like men they deserved the same rights, and insofar as they differed they ought to represent themselves (91).

Beginning in 1910, however, women from untoward areas, blacks, immigrants, political radicals, and college students joined the American woman suffrage movement. The word "feminism" was used for the first time to mean, as Charlotte Perkins Gilman put it, "the social awakening of the women of all the world" (1916), or, in Inez Milholland's words, to mean the "significant" and "profound movement to readjust the social position of women … in its largest general aspects" (1913, 181). The point is that from 1910 on, suffragists usually argued that women deserved the vote in spite of their sex.

With the Equal Rights Amendment there was a splintering of the women's movement. The ERA imbroglio brought to the surface the view, from the National Woman's Party, that women's capacities equaled those of men. They wanted to base their argument on the premise that the sexes were equal, since they saw sex equality as both possible and desirable. The great majority of women continued to stress their premise that women were weak and vulnerable, and that the world had to be accepted as it was, that is, a world of sex inequality. As Florence Kelley put it in 1921, "the cry Equality, Equality, where Nature has created Inequality, is as stupid and deadly as the cry Peace, Peace, where there is no Peace" (Cott 1986, 56).

Of course, in spite of the differences, there have also been remarkable periods of coalition building – 1912-1919 and 1967-1974. This seems to indicate that in spite of the factions that have existed, the social construction of womanhood does not prevent the building of "strategic evaluations," when instrumental or "expedient" reasons for advancing gender interests, that is, when characteristics or aims besides gender grievances, also motivate them (Cott, 1986, 59). In the women's movement, or movements, since 1970 or so, there has been a constant tension between those who stake out a claim for the power of sisterhood and the power of nonhegemonic groups, such as women of color and lesbians. Meanwhile, there has coexisted a feeling, a belief, that women are part of the general social order subject to political and cultural currents and are continuing to dispute whether feminism is a self-propagating or a sectarian ideology.

In Virility, a novella in her first collection of stories, Cynthia Ozick suggests that Elia Gatoff, who becomes Edmund Gate gains a writing STYLE that partook of the heathen colossus that had swelled to drive out everything callow – with his blunt and balding skull he looked … like a giant lingam: one of those curious phallic monuments one may suddenly encounter, wreathed with bright chains of leaves, on a dusty wayside in India" (Ozick 1983a, 244). Elia's fame, in short, is a product of his virility, which, in turn, leads to his poetry being described as "seminal and hard … Robust, lusty, male, Erotic" (Ozick 1983a, 254).

As Ozick wrote to me, in a letter dated 25 June 2003, "I've always thought that 'Virility' is even more a satiric/didactic feminist tract than it is a short story, so I was terrifically surprised to note … that one of your readers (of an early draft) actually asked 'Is Ozick a feminist?'"

Illustrative of this is Ozick's essay "Ruth" in which she offers her interpretation of *The Book of Ruth* (Ozick 1994). *The Book of Ruth*, we must recall, she asserts, is about exogamy, and not simple exogamy, such as marriage with a stranger or a member of a foreign culture. As a Moabite Ruth belonged to an enemy people, callous and pitiless, a people who dealt in lethal curses. How then to account for her presence in Israel's story? The Rabbis, in their infinite wisdom, ruled that a Moabite, not a Moabitess, was to be prohibited. The rabbis, after all, are symbolists and metaphor-seekers, moralists.

The result was that until Elimelech's death, Naomi, Ruth's mother, had followed her husband without question. Once her husband died, Naomi moved from the merely passive to "risks and contingencies well beyond the reach of comfortable common virtue" ("Ruth," 220). Suddenly, Naomi became – without warning or preparation – a woman of valor. The point is, as Ozick points out, "What we nowadays call feminism is of course as old as the oldest society imaginable; there have always been feminists; women (including the unsung) who will allow no element of themselves – gift, capacity, natural authority – to go unexpressed, whatever the weight of the mores" (in letter, 25 June, 2003).

Overnight, Naomi sets out on a program of autonomy. She will return to Bethlehem. Now, she says to her daughters-in-law, Ruth and Orpah: "Turn back, each of you to her mother's house. ... May the Lord grant that each of you find security in the house of a husband" ("Ruth," 221). Orpah, a loving young woman, is not an iconoclast; she goes home, or, rather, she stays home – which is why there is no Book of Orpah.

It falls to Ruth to set thirty centuries to trembling. Ruth replies: "Do not urge me to leave you, to turn back, and not follow you (Previsions of the Demist of the Dancing Dog, 1983b). After a year teaching supposedly talented undergraduates at a very good New York City university, she found that both male and female students were "alike in their illiteracy, undereducation, ignorance, and prejudice," and in their unshakable conviction that the writing, and even minds of "men and women are spectacularly unlike" (265).

"No one has been more serious and passionate, and certainly no one has been argumentative, concerning attitudes about women," Ozick wrote in 1965 (in Gornick 261), "when there was no glimmer of a woman's movement in sight." The rebels are few. Enlightenment has, for women, and especially by women, not yet occurred. In the mid-1960s, to write an essay on the exclusion (and self-exclusion) of women, was an anomalous and isolating act. Even the language then was strangely, unpleasantly formal. The gravity of tone, the temerity and mimicry, flaunted the sneer that feared a sneer. "Feminism was, in those years," Ozick recalled, "a private tenet one held alone, in an anarchic voice" (1983b, 261).

Cynthia Ozick's novella "*Usurpation*" offers an example of a narrative examining the nature of narrative. Here a woman author discovers the magical powers of the storyteller. According to Ozick, the novella is "a story written against storywriting, against the Muse-goddess, against Apollo" (1976); both the author and the author-figure are compelled by the powers offered the literary imagination. True, Ozick acknowledges the anti-Mosaic magic of literature and its compelling fascination for her, but she admits that "storytelling as every writer knows, is a magic art. Or Eucharist, wherein the common bread of language assumes the form of a god" (Preface, *Bloodshed*, 11). Significantly, in her "feminist" works, the women characters and narrators become social and spiritual models for women readers to emulate. On the one hand, as Claire Satloff (1983) shows, the stories present vivid portraits of women characters who succeed as women; on the other hand, in such stories by Ozick and others, the authors and their narrators and characters are also new archetypal "ancestors" with all that implies. In short, if women create the new myths, they are the Creators as well.

From this perspective, the new (post-1973) Jewish feminist fiction leads a trend in contemporary Jewish-American fiction away from the likes of Bellow, Malamud, and Roth, and toward what Ozick has termed "liturgical fiction" – a program that outlines Jewish preservation in America.

In an article written presumably in 1965, but first published in 1971, Cynthia Ozick devoted a year to "examining the minds of the young" ("Previsions," 263). All the characters were exactly the same age, and most had equal limitations of imagination and aspiration. Ozick was hired by a large urban university, in New York City, to teach English to freshmen: three classes of nearly a hundred young men and women, all seventeen, some city-born, some suburban, some well-off, some only scraping by, of every ethnic group and of every majority religion but Hindu. Almost all were equipped with "B" high-school averages; almost all were illiterate than not; almost all possessed similar prejudices expressed in identical platitudes. Almost all were tall, healthy, strong-toothed, obedient, and ignorant beyond their years. They had identical minuscule vocabularies, they were identically uneducated, and "the minds of the uneducated young women were identical to the minds of the uneducated young men" (263-64).

At that time it seemed axiomatic to Ozick that the minds of men and women were indistinguishable. The students confirmed this. As she saw it, what they all believed was this: "that minds of men and women are spectacularly unlike ... They believed that men write like men and women write like women. ... And they were all identical in this belief" (265). In this great university, in addition, she discovered that she was a "woman writer," and "that I was not a teacher, but a woman teacher" (266).

The point is that Ozick's colleagues distrusted her. She learned that every view she held was colored by sex. Their reasons for disliking Hemingway, for example, unlike hers, "were not taken to be simply ovarian." "In fact, both her students and her colleagues were equal adherents of the Ovarian Theory of Literature, or rather, its complement, the Testicular Theory" (266). Two cases in point: somewhere in a discussion about Flannery O'Connor's *Wise Blood*, Ozick referred to the author as "she." The class was astonished. They had not imagined that Flannery was a woman. Interestingly, one of the students, a very bright student, opined that she had known O'Connor was a woman: "Her sentences are a woman's sentences. … [T]hey're sentimental. … [T]hey're not concrete like a man's." The second example dealt with literature as physiology. One of her colleagues, insisting that style was influenced by physical makeup, proved his point by noting that Keats's poetry was affected by his having had tuberculosis. "Ah," Ozick put it to him cheerfully, "but you don't suppose, that being a woman is a *disease*?" (266-267).

Her colleague, of course, was a kindly sort and stuck to human matters: he did not mention dogs. On the other hand, many are aware of the remark upon hearing a woman preacher—she reminded him, he said, of a dog dancing on its hind legs; one marvels not a how well it is done, but that it can be done at all. "Two centuries, and the world of letters has not been altered by a syllable," writes Ozick, "unless you regard the switch from dogs to disease as a rudimentary advance. Perhaps it is. We have advanced so far that the dullest as well as the best of freshmen can scarcely be distinguished from Dr. Johnson, except by a bark" (268).

The Ovarian Theory of Literature, unfortunately, is the property of all society. A few years ago in *The New Yorker*, a critic, considering five novels, three of which were by women, began his review: "Women novelists, we have learned to assume, like to keep their focus narrow." Imagine. Beginning with, "we have learned to assume," he went on to praise and censure. He forgot or never knew that a woman is a person. She is not by the strength of her womb alone an artist. She can be an artist if she is born talented. Genius is the property of both sexes and all nations alike. The question then touches on all the human arts, including those we call science. In this context, woman will cease to be the man's muse when she ceases to be mused with gaudy daydreams and romances about her own nature. In fact, Ozick recalls, "I have heard her laughing at herself as though she were a dancing dog" (281).

Yes, the rebels are few. We tend to respect things as they are. An idea for its own sake, especially an obvious idea, has no respectability. Which is why, to come back to the students, according to Ozick, they could not write intelligibly. No one had ever mentioned the relevance of writing to thinking, and thinking had never been encouraged or induced in them. The obvious must not be permitted to thrust its scary beams. The "obvious," by the way, says Ozick, "means the gifts and teachings are life-illuminations of art." In a humanist society a voice will say, "Partake, live." You will one day reply, "How obvious," and if you laugh, "it will be the quaint folly of obsolete custom, which once failed to harness the obvious; it will not be at a dancing dog" (283).

Some ten years later, Cynthia Ozick, believing that this early essay was out of date, penned a new discussion: "Literature and the Politics of Sex: A Dissent" (1977). Although she wasn't sure, in 1983, whether the second essay was also out of date, she was quite sure in 2002 that it was both "a polemical piece" and "not at all dated." "(Not dated, but likely to be hated!)," as she wrote to me on July 3, 2002.

To begin with, Ozick writes that, "Women who write with an overriding consciousness that they write *as women* are engaged not in aspiration toward writing, but chiefly in a politics of sex." That is to say, "A new political term makes its appearance: *woman writer*, not used descriptively – 'as one would say, a lanky brown-haired writer' – but as part of the language of politics." In essence, the language of politics, she feels, is not writer's language. The political term "woman writer" signals in advance a whole set of premises: that there are "male" and "female" states of intellect and feeling, hence of prose; that individuality of condition and temperament do not apply or at least not much; that all writing women possess – not by virtue of being writers, but by virtue of being women – an instantly perceived common ground; and that writers who are women can best nourish other writers who are women (Ozick 1983b, 288).

Some have held that there is a human component to literature that a woman writer can more easily discuss with another woman writer, even across an ocean, than she can with the man next door. Ozick denies this vehemently. In her view there is a human component to literature that does not separate writers by sex, but on the contrary, engenders sympathies from sex to sex, from condition to condition, from experience to experience, from like to like, and from unlike to unlike. Without disparaging particular identities, it universalizes; it does not divide.

The traditional rabbinate, Ozick held (1979), tends to define feminist views as forms of selfishness, narcissism, and self-indulgence, all leading to what is always called "the breakdown of family life." But the sources of Jewish women's claims are more profound than that. It is not the upsurge of secular feminism that has caused the upsurge of Jewish feminism. For, having lost so much in the European cataclysm, the point is that Jewish women want equality as women with men, as Jews with Jews. The Talmud, for instance, as Adin Steinsaltz puts it, is the collective endeavor of the whole Jewish people. It is not then just the male half –

Jewish women have been purposely excised through the centuries – but the entire people. In the repair process there are women's Torah study groups, women's minyanim, and women's holiday celebrations. But until Jewish women are in the same relation to history and the Torah as men are and have been, Ozick holds, we should not allow ourselves ever again to indulge in the phrase "the Jewish genius" (*Lilith*, 250).

Of course, the pious ones state that women are dangerous temptations to men. In fact, observant Jewish men are without doubt better prepared than others for sexual restraint; it is not pious Jewish males who are weak in the face of women – only their arguments. Another scandal separates Jews from the Covenant, because, writes Ozick, "the issue of the status of Jewish women flows from societal, not sacral, sources." What this derives from is the Torah's "certainty and immutability of certain moral principles, beyond social custom and even despite nature" (*Lilith*, 144-46).

It is no use saying the world is not like this. The point of the Commandments is that the world is not like that, the Commandments are contrary to the way the world is – with one exception: at the start of the Creation of the World, woman is given an inferior place, a position of lesserness, with an "assumption of inferiority," that is, of "dehumanization." There is no "Thou shalt not lessen the inferiority of women" in Torah. Thus, there is a need, concludes Ozick, to strengthen Torah, to contradict injustice, to create justice – through the cleansing precept of justice itself, so that our progeny, ages hence, will look back and say "what was done was done in accordance with the voice of the Covenant." It is necessary for the sake of women, of course, but it is necessary also "for the sake of Torah: to preserve and strengthen Torah itself" (*Lilith*, 151).

So what is a woman writer? Outside of its political uses, Ozick claims, "woman writer" has no meaning. To her, "a writer is a writer." Does a woman writer have a separate psychology? She asks. Does a woman writer have a separate body of ideas? It is misleading currencies that "classical feminism" was created to bring an end to. In art, the imagination cannot be "set" free, because it is already free. To say the imagination is free, writes Ozick (1977), is a tautology. "The imagination is by definition, by nature, freedom and autonomy. When I write, I am free. I am, as a writer, whatever I wish to become. ... In life, I am not free. In life, female or male, no one is free. In life, female or male, I have tasks; I have obligations and responsibilities" ("Literature and the Politics of Sex," 285). Indeed, "When I write, I am in command of a grand *As If.* I write *As If* I were truly free. And this *As If* is not a myth. As soon as I proclaim it, as soon as my conduct as a writer expresses it, it comes into being" (287).

Simply put, classical feminism – i.e., feminism at its origin, when it saw itself as justice and aspiration made universal, as mankind widened to humankind – rejected anatomy not only as destiny, but as any sort of governing force; it interjected the notion of "female sensibility" as a slander designed to shut women off from access to the delights, confusions, achievements, darknesses, and complexities of the great world. Classical feminism was concerned with the end of false barriers and boundaries; with the end of segregationist fictions and restraints; with the end of the Great Multiple Lie. Classical feminism, while not denying the body, while not precluding self-image and self-knowledge, never dreamed of engaging these as single-minded objectives. For writers who are women, the "new-truth" of self-regard, of biologically based self-confinement, is the Great Multiple Lie got up in drag.

For writers there are no new truths. There is only one very old truth, as old as Sappho, as old as Homer, as old as the Song of Deborah, as old as the Songs of David – that the imagination is free. What we ought to do then, Ozick holds, is not wait for freedom, meanwhile idling in self-analyses; the freedom one waits for, as writers, is to seize freedom now, immediately, by recognizing that we already have it (294).

REFERENCES

Cott, Nancy. 1986. "Feminist theory and feminist movements: The past before us." In *What is Feminism?* Ed. Juliet Mitchell and Ann Oakley. Oxford: Blackwell.

Gilman, Charlotte Perkins. 1916. "What Is Feminism?" *Boston Sunday Herald*, 3 September.

Gornick, Vivian and Barbara K. Moran, eds. 1971. *Women in Sexist Society: Studies in Power and Powerlessness*. New York: Basic Books.

Kraditor, Aileen. 1965. *The Ideas of the Women Suffrage Movement 1890-1920*. New York: Columbia University Press.

Milholland, Inez. 1913. "The Liberation of a Sex." *McClure's*, February, 181.

Ozick, Cynthia. 1976. "Preface." In *Bloodshed and Three Novellas*. New York: Knopf.

-. 1977. "Literature and the Politics of Sex: A Dissent." *Ms.*, December, 284-94. Reprinted in Cynthia Ozick. *Art and Ardor* (New York: Knopf, 1983).

-. 1979. "Notes Toward Finding the Right Question." *Lilith Magazine*, No. 6, 120-51.

-. 1983a. *The Pagan Rabbi and Other Stories*. New York: Dutton.

-. 1983b. "Previsions of the demise of the dancing dog." In *Art and Ardor*. New York: Knopf. First published in *Women in Sexist Society: Studies in Power and Powerlessness*, ed. Vivian Gornick and Barbara K. Moran (New York: Basic Books, 1971).

-. 1994. "Ruth." In *Reading Ruth: Contemporary Women Reclaim a Sacred Story*, ed. Judith Kates and Gail T. Reimer. New York: Ballantine.

-. 1997. "The Many Faces of Cynthia Ozick." Interview with Katie Bolick in *Atlantic Online*, http://www.theatlantic.com/unbound/factfict/ozick.htm, 15 may.

Satlof, Claire. 1983. "History, Fiction and the Tradition: Creating a Jewish Feminist Poetic." In *On Being a Jewish Feminist*, ed. Susannah Heschel. New York: Schocken.

6. Waiting for Moshiach

Reading Absence in Ozick's *The Messiah of Stockholm*

Jessica Lang

In a quoted preface to *The Messiah of Stockholm*, Cynthia Ozick gives the reader a citation from Bruno Schulz's *The Street of Crocodiles*—the Polish title is *Cinnamon Shops*: "My father never tired of glorifying this extraordinary element—matter. 'There is no dead matter,' he taught us, 'lifelessness is only a disguise behind which hide unknown forms of life. The range of these forms is infinite and their shades and nuances limitless...'" The citation not only serves as the animating spirit to Ozick's work, it functions as an uncanny reminder of Schulz's legacy as an author and artist and also the legacy of serving as a muse to so many other authors. Cynthia Ozick, David Grossman, and Philip Roth are among the more well-known novelists who bring Bruno Schulz as a figure into their fiction; other scholars make a convincing case that authors Danilo Kis and Tadeusz Kantor reflect Schulz's influence through "figures and icons" in their own work.[2] Grossman notes about *See: Under Love* that he "wanted to write a book that would tremble on the shelf. That would equal the blink of an eye in a man's life – not 'life' in the tedious, passage-of-time sense; not 'life' as subjugated vassal of the evanescence and tyranny of nature; but the 'life' that Schulz's writing showed me: life's life. Life in spades. Not a life that is satisfied with or proud of merely not having murdered the Other, but a life that settles for nothing less than the Other's revival, for nothing less that the revival of the moment just past, of things seen a thousand times before, of that word, of me, of you."[3] Whether relying on Schulz's own words, or reflecting on Schulz's influence in their own work, the powerful effect of Schulz's work, known for its ethereal, almost ghostly, magical quality, and the brutality of his murder, clearly inspire a longing to somehow re-animate his spirit, his voice and, in doing so, recognize and amplify his literary, and more broadly artistic, contributions.

In 1941, when the Germans moved into Shulz's hometown of Drohobycz, an SS officer named Felix Landau, who had an interest in art, recognized Schulz's talent and, in return for extra food and the promise of protection, ordered a range of paintings from Schulz, among them a series of murals depicting scenes from well-known fairy tales for his son's bedroom. On November 19, 1942, hours before Schulz was planning to flee from the ghetto of Drohobycz where all Jews had been forced to re-locate, he was shot in the streets by an SS officer angry at Landau for having earlier killed a Jewish man under his protection. According to several eyewitnesses, this officer declared to Landau shortly afterwards: "You killed my Jew—I killed yours."[4] (Other sources have disputed this version, noting that a massacre in Drohobycz on November 19, 1942 resulted in the deaths of over 200 Jews in the ghetto; Schulz's death may have been a part of this larger tragedy.)

In real terms, Schulz's literary and artistic legacy was established by remarkably little: at the time of his death he had self-published a series of his drawings in a collection entitled "The Book of Idolatry" (around 1921) and he exhibited some of his artwork publicly in Warsaw, Lvov, Vilna, and Cracow. Schulz published two books of short stories during his lifetime, *Cinnamon Shops* (1934) and *Sanatorium Under the Sign of the Hourglass* (1937). *Cinnamon Shops* was written while Schulz taught art in the public school of Drohobycz, where he himself had graduated about 15 years earlier. He began teaching there in 1924, when he was 32 years old, unable to support himself otherwise. *Cinnamon Shops* brought him literary fame and acknowledgement, winning a prestigious prize in 1935 and contributing to his Golden Laurel award from the Polish Academy of Literature in 1938. His literary voice has been connected to writers as various as Franz Kafka, the Polish Romantic poet Adam Mickiewicz, Marcel Proust, and even Henry James and James Joyce.

Schulz's legacy, however, has been as much informed by what has been read and published as it has been by that which is known to have been lost. Schulz, in an attempt to ensure that his work would be safe, towards the end of his life entrusted different portions of his papers with different people, at least one of whom has gone unidentified, along with the papers entrusted to him. Included among the cache of lost materials are: Schulz's only work written in German; a novella entitled *Die Heimkehr*; stories; fragments; a vast quantity of letters; diaries maintained over the course of many years; and a great many sketches, drawings, and graphic works. Most elusive and most tantalizing among this cache is the unfinished manuscript of a novel entitled *Messiah*, about which Schulz wrote from time to time in salvaged letters to friends. "*Messiah* grows slowly," he wrote to a friend in 1934; "You touched a sensitive spot, asking about my *Messiah*. I'm getting nowhere with it," he wrote in 1936.[5] During the war Schulz read portions of *Messiah* aloud to friends, one of whom remembers the central theme of the novel as revolving around a "'return to childhood' and 'messianic times'".[6] The absence of Bruno's *Messiah*, which would have substantially enlarged Schulz's oeuvre, has become a touchstone for authors and artists, at least in part because the absent novel, with its enormous and tantalizing promise, makes both material and immaterial the murder of Schulz himself. Grossman writes that once he "met a man who said Bruno Schulz had shown him the first line: morning rising over a city; a certain light; towers. No one ever saw more. This private myth was buried; perhaps one day it will resurface as a grain of sand, the fragment of an idol."[7] Ruth Franklin notes that Schulz's works "have an inherent ephemerality, vanishing almost as soon as they are experienced...They exist for just one glorious instant, made all the more beautiful by the impossibility of their reconstruction."[8] An essential aspect of Schulz's legacy resides not only in the texts themselves, but in the cracks and fissures, some running deep and far, that separate the reader from his prose.

I turn now to an analysis of Ozick's *The Messiah of Stockholm*, in which the discovery of the book after which the novel is named, Schulz's *Messiah*, results in a terrifying combination of meaning and, simultaneously, its complete and utter absence, a reflection of the text we can handle, namely Ozick's, and the one we have been deprived of—Schulz's. In an interview where she writes that she deliberately never resolves the questions of whether the manuscript in *The Messiah of Stockholm*, claimed to be Schulz's *Messiah*, is actually authentic. Instead, Ozick says, "I simply leave that to the reader. I obfuscated it in layer after layer after layer…"[9] Building on that sense of obfuscation, here I propose that the act of discovering meaning, which is really at the heart of the Schulz citation at the beginning of *The Messiah of Stockholm*, is for Ozick an act of reading, although a highly problematized one. By reading, I do not mean the mechanical process associated with basic literacy. Instead, I understand the nature of reading for Ozick to be one that about experiencing a relationship with and to the text. And here is the problem at the heart of *The Messiah of Stockholm* and one that much of Ozick's Holocaust fiction grapples with, namely that reading requires text; body; matter. In the case of Schulz's *Messiah*, we have been denied that physical form, an act of dispossession that Ozick struggles to quantify and describe: for there is no dead matter, to return to the opening words of her book, only unknown forms of life and so the question is how to make sense or meaning—in short, how to read—that which has disappeared.

Indeed, in a gesture nearly parallel to that of Ozick and other authors who bring Schulz back to life in their fiction, Schulz's lost work also keeps reasserting itself, through rumor but also through fact, returning to the eternal nature of "matter" that Ozick references and the "life's life" described by Grossman. The most recent example of this is with the frescoes that Schulz was forced to paint on the walls of the nursery occupied by Landau's young son. In 2001 a German film director, Benjamin Geissler, interested in recovering these murals did just that, discovering them in spite of the layers of paint and other renovations that hid them from view for decades. The ensuing controversy over ownership rights of the murals, with Yad Vashem squirreling some fragments out of the country in May 2001 and with Ukrainian officials claiming theft of a cultural and national treasure, has to some degree obscured the remarkable nature of the artwork itself, namely a series of fairy-tale images that were painted with the faces and characteristics of members from Drohobycz's local and imperiled Jewish community. One of Schulz's former students, Emil Górski, assisted Schulz and decades later, remembering the images, wrote: "We painted scenes from fairy tales—Schulz sketched the composition in its entirety, and I painted certain details. And here Schulz remained somehow faithful to his creative principle: in the paintings on the wall of the child's room, in the fantastic fairy-tale scenery, the characters of kings, knights, squires had the completely 'un-Aryan' features of the faces of people among whom Schulz lived at the time. Their similarity to the emaciated and tortured faces that Schulz had captured in memory was extraordinary. Here these tormented people—transported through Schulz's imagination from the world of tragic reality—found for themselves in paintings brilliant richness and pride; as kings on thrones in sable furs, with golden crowns on their heads; on beautiful white horses as knights in armor, with swords in their hands and surrounded by knights; seated lie powerful lords in golden carriages."[10]

In spite of the fact that these images, and the story behind them, were discovered well over a decade after *The Messiah of Stockholm* was published, in many ways they coincide neatly with the story Ozick both makes available to readers, and the one that she sets up purposely to elude us. First: the interrogation of the art itself. Before the war Schulz regularly accepted commissions and assignments for various kinds of art projects for extra income, although he never viewed these works as true art or considered them part of his portfolio. While the ominous circumstances around the Landau "commission" (the transaction implied by the word hardly begins to describe the true nature of the exchange) certainly made the necessity of completing the murals of an entirely different nature, precisely this difference in origin is embodied in the work. Like other commissioned pieces, Schulz never viewed the frescoes as true art and yet used the narrative he was forced to deliver to depict, at least in part, a narrative he truly wanted to tell, one about his home, his neighbors, his family—the place and characters that populate all of his works, written and visual. (Indeed, former students of Schulz describe the strange fairy tales that he would sometimes narrate to the class, illustrating them as he went along on the blackboard. One student described them as revolving around "'a child, his adventures, his sometimes strange fate.'"[11]) One may even move a step further and make the case that presenting local Drohobycz Jews in carriages and as kings is a form of deliverance, one that is both a "'return to childhood'" and an illustration of "'messianic times'"—the two fragmented descriptions left us of Schulz's *Messiah*.

Second to the art itself is its discovery and reclamation. Scholar Norman Ravvin takes issue with "Schulz-centred books" such as those produced by Ozick and Grossman, understanding them as a "persistent reinscription of Schulz's death," one that effectively deprives him of an afterlife because they identify him almost entirely by his murder, making Schulz's death "a point of fascination."[12] And yet I understand both the fiction inspired by Shulz and the interest in visiting the exhibit of Schulz's murals as stemming from the same tension, namely that separating the competing claims between history and art, between victim and visionary. In 2009, eight years after some fragments of the mural were spirited out of Landau's former home, the Yad Vashem Holocaust museum opened its exhibition around them entitled "Wall Painting Under Coercion." A wide array of newspapers and articles, in English, Hebrew and Ukrainian, addressed the complex dialogue between claiming and belonging in connection to the murals and what the murals have come to stand for, namely Schulz's art and, indeed, even his identity. In a clear effort to mend some of the tears generated by removing the fragments from their place of origin, the Yad Vashem exhibit includes the sentence: "The paintings are on long-term loan from the Drohobychyna Museum, Ukraine." The interest in questions of ownership work in a strange way to illustrate the element of not merely life but also afterlife that Schulz's work, both artistic and literary, achieves. "The range of these forms is infinite," he notes and Ozick repeats, "and their shades and nuances limitless…"

The last uncanny connection between Schulz's work on Landau's walls, its afterlife as a museum exhibit, and the presence that Schulz exerts in contemporary fiction revolves around form. The Yad Vashem exhibit is one that centers on fragments, a word that perhaps best describes not only this but many of Schulz's works. Both of his published books, *Cinnamon Shops* and *Sanatorium Under the Sign of the Hourglass*, are collections of short stories. And while each story is complete, each one often conveys an ethereality that lifts it from conventional markers such as time, place and form. Franklin notes the "magical transformations and moments outside time" that take place in his stories. Rolando Perez notes the element of "quiet anxiety about the fate of material existence" that pervades Schulz's work, a quality that, on the one hand, lends his art and stories a sense of doom and masochism, and, on the other, moves them beyond the worldly and the bodily, establishing them as transcendent, mythical and eternal.[13] Schulz's completed stories hold a glimpse within them his incomplete works--indeed, at least a few of his short stories are thought to be fragments from the lost works. And then even our knowledge of these lost works—that they existed and that Schulz struggled to continue them; that he treasured them enough to want to save them; that he shared some elements and some chapters of these works with others—all of these qualities contribute to not only the fragmentariness of the works themselves but also to Schulz himself, a figure whose own fragmented artistic identity was imposed on him brutally—murderously even—but also was self-described in his own work: "And yet, in a certain sense, the fullness is contained wholly and integrally in each of [the Book's] crippled and fragmentary incarnations. An event may be small and insignificant in its origins and yet, when drawn close to one's eye, it may open in its centre an infinite and radiant perspective because a higher order or being is trying to express itself in it and irradiates it violently. Thus we shall collect these allusions, these earthly approximations, these stations and stages on the paths of our life, like the fragments of a broken mirror".[14] For Schulz, fragments have the unexpected and even paradoxical effect of lending a sense of wholeness to image and objective. And this is because fragments not only include the art itself, textual or pictoral, but also the space around it, which cuts into it, defining the work's limits but also intimating that its limits are unknown and, through this unknowing, limitless.

In "The Mythologizing of Reality," Schulz writes that each "fragment of reality lives by virtue of partaking in a universal Sense...The word in its common usage today is only a fragment, remnant of some former all-embracing, integral mythology. That is why it possesses a tendency to grow back, to regenerate and complete itself in full meaning."[15] To return to Ozick's *The Messiah of Stockholm*, the novel is her solution to reading the fragmentariness of Schulz's work both in its singular form—the lost book *Messiah*—and in its broadest iteration—Schulz's life.[16] The problem or question of reading text that we know exists and so can physically handle, pass on, turn the pages of and so on, as compared to that text which we know exists but we *cannot* handle, ultimately attaches itself to the act of what I call unreading. Unreading is a textual quality in which the relationship achieved between text and reader is called into question and unable to develop. Unreading refers to an aspect or element of failed understanding on the part of the reader—a failure that is the product of the text reaching certain limits in the range of experiences or definitions that are the tools used by most readers to access and understand text. In this sense, unreading identifies a quality of inaccessibility that borders on blankness or even illegibility—moments when a text's meaning simply cannot be truly processed and understood, regardless of the apparatus or methodology that is applied.

In Ozick's *The Messiah of Stockholm*, unreading enables readers to acknowledge that a text like Schulz's *Messiah* exists – it is, was and always will be and will have presence and matter -- and yet at the same time we are unable to define the text or know its specific qualities. Whereas reading is in many ways a transgressive act where characters, themes and ideas are appropriated, internalized, and affiliated, unreading resists these gestures and remains, importantly and even profoundly, impervious to them.

The Messiah of Stockholm centers on Lars Andemening, a World War II refugee from Poland who has been raised in Sweden by a foster family. Lars has invented an elaborate history for himself, one he is firmly committed to: he is the unknown and unidentified son of Bruno Schulz. In an interview, Ozick declares that Lars is the ultimate forger. "He's forged his own life. He's forged his own identity. He has no idea of who he was…and he's struggling for an identity which by definition can only be negative. It's an identity which can be pursued only through negation, through murder, through annihilation."[17] Lars's dogged attempts to discover his father's lost manuscript, *Messiah*, can also be read and understood as a wish to be reunited with his past; if Schulz is his father, then the *Messiah* is his brother. To read it is to know what has long been hidden; to hold it is to confirm its 'matter,' its very nature, and, consequently, Andemening's own. Lars and the other characters that populate *The Messiah of Stockholm* feed the elusive dream-like quality of the novel, itself a reflection of Schulz's influence as well as an elegy to him. "There is no dead matter" in the novel, surely, but its hidden "unknown forms of life" bear phantasmagorical qualities—an aspect of the text that Ozick may well have borrowed from Schulz's *Cinnamon Shops*—that make meaning hard to pin down in any form, both that within the discovered manuscript by Schulz but also that of the story we as readers hold in our hands. This element of something-but-nothing, there-but-not-there, extends to the various artefacts and idiosyncratic characters that populate the tale. Among them are the shopkeeper Heidi Eklund, the bookshop owner who carries Schulz books, and her mysterious near-invisible husband, Dr. Eklund. Heidi introduces Lars to Adela, a woman who claims not only to have a copy of Schulz's *Messiah* in her possession, but also to be Schulz's daughter. Both of these claims are viewed with the utmost skepticism by Lars and by us, the other readers, but are endorsed by the Eklunds, who, it gradually emerges, are Adela's parents.

Ultimately, *The Messiah of Stockholm* is a deeply ambivalent text, as revealed not only by the treatment of text within the novel but also by our own experience of reading it: what is the alliance between the Eklunds and Adela that subject the reader to their whims and fancy? Are we to believe that the manuscript is authentically Schulz's? How would such a discovery transform Lars's world, one defined by his relationship to Schulz? What effect would it have on our world, that belonging to the secondary set of readers? In posing these and other questions, the novel swings from moments that are bizarre and surreal to others that are humorous and rather ordinary and to others still that are devastatingly tragic. Naomi Sokoloff rightly notes that *The Messiah of Stockholm* "is a novel that disallows the validity of plot and invention in a context devoid of referential certainty…While the text presents its main character clearly as idea, it employs a proliferation of wild metaphors and a language sometimes abruptly divorced from the objects of representation. Both features emerge out of the underlying concern of the text with invention and with fiction as spurious make-believe."[18] The tension between fiction and history is heightened through Ozick play on names, relationships and authorship. Adela is the name of the housekeeper in Schulz's *Cinnamon Shops* and Ozick's amphora-stuffed-with-manuscript-carrying mock heroine; Schulz's father, the subject of many stories in *Cinnamon Shops*, is literalized in *The Messiah of Stockholm* through Lars Andemening, who, although he convinces himself that he is the son of Schulz, could just as easily be the son of Dr. Eklund, a figure who remains an invisible reference until the last part of the novel, his ghostly presence asserting itself through absence more than through presence. The cross-pollination between multiple historical and fictional worlds has the simultaneous and contradictory effect of both drawing them closer together, integrating the ordinary with art and beauty of the highest order, and also pulling them apart, forcing readers to identify the two very separate worlds and what each has to offer.

With the exception of the reading of Schulz's *Messiah*, reading in *The Messiah of Stockholm* is positioned as both ordinary and necessary. And this is partly Ozick's point: namely, that the reading and revelation of Schulz's *Messiah* falls out of time, out of place and out of meaning. Reading can and should be a daily activity, one that is essential and important enough to draw minute descriptions from the narrator. Lars, the protagonist of *The Messiah of Stockholm*, "reads [Polish] with a clumsy tongue, but a lightning eye, in pursuit of his father's tales" (5). Lars is a more fluent reader of the books he reviews professionally for a local paper: "In the morning he read. This meant that he started on the first page and finished on the last. He was not a skimmer or a sniffer; he read meticulously, as if, swimming, he were being filmed in slow motion. The text swept him away and consumed him—he was like a man (the man in the bedclothes in his father's tale) drawn down by an undertow. Slowly, slowly, the imaginary cinema recorded his heavy resisting gulps. Reading was as exhausting to him as the long, weighted strokes of a drowning man. He gave it all his power. Then he cooked himself a bowl of farina and fell into the wilderness of his quilt." (8) Within the novel, acts of reading occur with regular periodicity and encompass an experience—every morning Lars reads passionately and exhaustively. Reading Schulz's *Messiah*, however, is to read a book whose history has rendered it permanently elusive—and this even as Lars holds it in his hands, even as he parses its words.

Twice divorced and separated by continents from his only child, Lars develops his own sense of time and ritual in the seclusion of his tiny apartment. His identification as a lost son, his search for the lost manuscript, his work writing obscure book reviews, have a peculiar backwards pull, creating a sense of undoing as he ages, rather than doing, of devolving rather than evolving, of regressing rather than maturing. He is forty-two years old when the novel opens but "looked much younger, probably because he was spare and showed bone…But also there was something in his face that opened into unripeness—a tentativeness, an unfinished tone…He was often dealt with as if he was just starting out, heaving his greening masculine forces against life" (3-4). Lars's foreignness in the novel—he is not a native Swede but, more than that, he just doesn't fit in anywhere—is one of the text's most American qualities. At a remove from his Eastern European ancestors, Lars lives a solitary existence all the while trying to connect and re-connect to those around him and before him. His isolation in many ways reflects the sense present in other American Holocaust imaginative works of being too far removed, too distant, to be able to write or know of what happened during World War II. Indeed, his very name, Andamening, suggests not only his desire to uncover signs—to create 'meaning'-, but to add it to what already exists—"and a meaning". Through the recognition of inheritance and lineage, Lars longs to determine the indeterminate, to give form to matter, and the path he chooses to do this is by recognizing and celebrating a work of art whose invisibility has elevated it to a near mythic status. Lars wants to find that work of art, that text, and through reading create a sense of memory for it, build it a past that will resonate with his own, one that is specific – held fast by words -- and cumulative, bearing the weight of family and Jewish history.

And yet Ozick's uneasiness with the elevation of art above all else is well-documented. In her preface to *Bloodshed*, Ozick notes that the "story-making faculty itself can be a corridor to the corruptions and abominations of idol-worship, of the adoration of magical event."[19] Ozick pursues this line of thinking in her essay "Literature as Idol: Harold Bloom" where she accuses Bloom of "breaking off with the precursor," of violating that which "has been transmitted; a deliberate offense against the given, against the hallowed; an unhallowing of the old great gods... Above all, the theft of power."[20] Ozick's wariness regarding the elevation of art above all else does not stop her from engaging in a great deal of witty play in *The Messiah of Stockholm*—Lars's quest for *Messiah* is at once a search for the Holy Grail—literally—at one point the manuscript is stored in a brass amphora. But Ozick is also reluctant, as one might expect, to turn storytelling, or in this case story reading, into idol worship, a transformation of the text into "a graven image."[21] Stories, Ozick writes, can become "a corridor to the corruptions and abominations of idol worship, of the adoration of the magical event." Her deeply held convictions regarding fiction-as-idolatry are further complicated by her equally entrenched (and well-publicized) reluctance to include the Holocaust in fiction, her insistence that depictions of the Holocaust "ought to remain exclusively attached to document and history." This belief is partnered with her recognition regarding her own work that even if she does not "want to tamper or invent or imagine [around the Holocaust]...I have done it. I can't not do it. It comes. It invades."[22] Ozick has repeatedly reiterated both the strength of her intellectual position—"I'm against writing Holocaust fiction"—and the force exerted by art: "And yet, for some reason, I keep writing Holocaust fiction. It is something that has happened to me; I can't help it."[23]

Unlike other quests for holy objects, and here I am thinking broadly of American stories that struggle with the elevation of art against a backdrop of sin, crime, or some kind of offense -- Hawthorne's scarlet letter and Bartleby's originality; James's portrait and Bellow's Chicago -- unlike these texts, Ozick's novel does not stop with the discovery of the thing itself. Rather, meaning and objectification become quickly divorced. Instead of celebrating "it"—the long sought-after manuscript that is discovered decades after Schulz's brutal murder—Ozick pushes further, pursuing on behalf of all readers the far more elusive goal of meaning and, even more specifically, meaning through reading. Lars does not so much as read the text of *The Messiah* as fall into it "with the force of a man who throws himself against a glass wall…Lars did not resist or hide; he let his flesh rip. Nothing detained him, nothing slowed him down. The terrible speed of his hunger, chewing through hook and blade, tongue and voice, of the true Messiah! Rapacity, gluttony!" (105) And yet, even as he reads, he fails to read. Lars could "not contain what he met; he could not keep it. Amnesia descended with the opacity of a dropped hood. What he took he lost. And instantly grieved, because he could not keep it" (106). The act of reading is not the only inaccessible feature of *Messiah*; textuality itself is thrown into disarray, the "poor battered sheets [are] erratically paginated" and some are "not numbered at all…" They flow one "into another; there were sequences and consequences, parallels and paradoxes, however you shuffled them." "[T]he order of the pages did not matter" (106). The "intelligence" of *Messiah* is described as "voluminously overlapping, everything simultaneous and multiform" and yet, the narrator cautions us, "this understanding applied only to a consciousness of system. *The Messiah* was a waterless tract" (106). [I]nsofar as [*Messiah*] could be determined to be 'about' anything…[it] was about creation and redemption. It was a work of cosmogony and entelechy…*The Messiah*," the narrator tells us, "had its 'locality,' its place, its inch, its spot of tiny ground," namely Drohobycz. After giving us this one detail, something happens to the narrator's attempt to describe more specifically the contents of *Messiah*. There is a shift where we, the readers of *The Messiah of Stockholm*, can no longer tell if the narrator is describing the imagined contents of Schulz's *Messiah* or a version of the book's history, replete with the destruction and conflagration that is somewhat familiar to us because it is part of the history of Schulz, it is the history of the Holocaust. This description concludes with the recognition of only a single survivor remaining, "an organism called the Messiah" (111). That word is not italicized; it's not the text that the narrator refers to there, but rather a "small beating bird," a minute form of life disguised behind "dead matter." Texuality, Ozick implies, with all its associations with and ties to object and body, is important, particularly in relation to the Holocaust, but recognizing the absence of text, and with it the unavailability of meaning, may be an even more powerful form of remembering. For all of her playfulness around notions of art and idolatry, between forgery and authenticity, between the web of relationships linking Lars, Schulz, the two Adelas, and the two Eklunds, in short, between historical fact and the postmodern imagination, Ozick pares down

In the conclusion to her essay "Who Owns Anne Frank?," first published in *The New Yorker* in 1997, ten years after *The Messiah of Stockholm* came out, Ozick writes that while it "may be shocking to think this…one can imagine a still more salvational outcome: Anne Frank's diary burned, vanished, lost—saved from a world that made of it all things, some of them true, while floating lightly over the heavier truth of named and inhabited evil." A few years after Ozick writes these highly contested lines, Schulz's murals are discovered and the scuffle and jostling over the rights of memory, art and history ensues. In quiet contrast stands *The Messiah of Stockholm*, where Ozick gives space to the fantasy and near-sacred promise of absence. Schulz's *Messiah* has been found in Ozick's novel, engulfed by a ferocious appetite of reading and attachment, and then Lars, the reader, puts a match to the pages housed in the brass amphora making it turn black: "it wobbled, sputtered, expired; it smoked and smoked" (127). The holy grail becomes the chimneys of Auschwitz and the text, the *Messiah*, with all its promise of redemption, does not survive. What remains for Lars is not a word or an idea, but its smell as it burns, a smell that disappears and reappears "in the blue light of Stockholm," one that is sufficient to jog his memory of the existence of text and body, one that remains crucially beyond reach, beyond reading, and yet one that truly matters.

David Goldfarb, "A Living Schulz: Noc wielkiego sezonu" ("The Night of the Great Season"). http://www.echonyc.com/~goldfarb/schulz/htm in Norman Ravvin, "Veneration and Desecration: The Afterlife of Bruno Schulz," *Bruno Schulz: New Readings, New Meanings* (Montreal: Polish Institute of Arts and Sciences in Canada, 2009) 56.

The Collected Works of Bruno Schulz, Edited by Jerzy Ficowski (New York: Picador, 1998) vii.

Jerzy Ficowski, *Regions of the Great Heresy: Bruno Schulz: A Biographical Portrait*, Translated and Edited by Theodosia Robertson (New York: W.W. Norton & Company, 2003) 138.

Fikowski 147-8.

Fikowski 148.

The Collected Works of Bruno Schulz, vii.

Ruth Franklin, "The Lost: Searching for Bruno Schulz," *The New Yorker*, "Books," 16 December 2002.

Mario Materassi and Cynthia Ozick, "Imagination Unbound: An Interview with Cynthia Ozick," *Salmagundi* 94/95 (1992): 100.

Ficowski 166-7.

Ficowski 49.

Ravvin 58.

Rolando Perez, *Bruno Schulz: Literary Kabbalist of the Holocaust: An Anne Bass Schneider Lecture in Jewish Social Studies* (New York: Hunter College of the City University of New York, 2002) 10-18.

The Collected Works of Bruno Schulz, "The Book," 111.

Letters and Drawings of Bruno Schulz with Selected Prose, Edited by Jerzy Ficowski (New York: Fromm International Publishing Corporation, 1990) 115.

Indeed, Ozick herself confesses to resisting reading and re-reading Schulz or facts about his biography during the writing of *The Messiah of Stockholm*, limiting herself to about four pages of "biographical matter" that she "read obsessively again and again" while refusing to read the text of Schulz's stories while actively writing her own. Materassi and Cynthia Ozick, 104.

Mario Materassi and Cynthia Ozick, 100-101.

Naomi Sokoloff, "Reinventing Bruno Schulz: Cynthia Ozick's "The Messiah of Stockholm" and David Grossman's "See Under: Love," *AJS Review* 13 (1988): 179.

Cynthia Ozick, *Bloodshed and Three Novellas* (NY: Knopf Press, 1976) 11.

Cynthia Ozick, *Art & Ardor* (New York: Alfred A. Knopf, 1983) 185.

Elisabeth Rose explores effectively Ozick's integration of art and monotheism in: Elisabeth Rose, Cynthia Ozick's Liturgical Postmodernism: *The Messiah of Stockholm*," *Studies in American Jewish Literature* 9 (1990): 93-107.

Elaine M. Kauvar, "An Interview with Cynthia Ozick," *Contemporary Literature* 34 (1993): 390.

Katie Bolick, *Atlantic Unbound: Interviews*, "The Many Faces of Cynthia Ozick," *The Atlantic Online*, 15 May 1997. http://www.theatlantic.com/past/docs/unbound/factfict/ozick.htm

7. Interview with Cynthia Ozick

Jane Statlander-Slote and Alessandra Farkas

AF: Will the theme of the Holocaust always somehow be present in your writings?

CO: So it seems, even against my will. Though surely not in everything I've written; for instance, some time ago I found pleasure and relief in a comic novella, called *Dictation*, about the mischievous collusion of two amanuenses, one secretary to Henry James, the other to Joseph Conrad. But very soon afterward, as I resumed work on *Foreign Bodies*, a novel, I was taken by surprise — once again a survivor turned up, this time of Transnistria. I neither wanted her nor expected her, and there she suddenly was. In principle (a principle I have violated) I am not in favor of the fictionalization or mythopoeticization of the Holocaust; the documents speak graphically and bitterly enough.

Yet it will never be possible — it has never been possible — to escape the effect of this mammoth atrocity of the twentieth century, which has changed the world forever. Changed the world forever, you may ask, when time obliterates nearly everything? And new atrocities mount? But sometimes time doesn't obliterate; sometimes it deforms, and in deforming history, it teaches replication. Indeed, it inspires replication. "Never again," that noble slogan, has been hideously transmogrified into "Of course again! Since it was done before, and so easily done without meaningful opposition, what's to stop us from doing it again?" A lesson not lost on Adolf Hitler: "Who, after all," he notoriously said (and we are not often enough reminded that he said it), "speaks today of the annihilation of the Armenians?" Hence Rwanda; hence Darfur; hence the mullahs of Iran, their proxies, their jihadist clones, their sympathizers and cynical abettors, among whom are., notoriouisly, the UN so-called Human Rights Council and Turkey's Tayyip Erdogan.

And there is more. The Holocaust has produced crocodile tears everywhere, no more so than in Europe, the staging ground for the mass abduction and mass murder of Jews. The Holocaust has become a fig leaf for Europe's resurgent anti-Semitism under its new mask, anti-Zionism (just as, historically, the term anti-Semitism, with its linguistic overtones, was a new mask for open Jew-hatred). Think of all those solemn memorials for dead Jews on a Sunday afternoon, while on Monday morning the same pious speechmakers devise brutish assaults on living Jews in a mercilessly besieged Israel. At such times there is little to choose between the speechifiers and the deniers. Which is why the Holocaust, used and abused by the criers of crocodile tears, is today more in my mind than ever. Lili, the survivor character in *Foreign Bodies*, has a name for Europe: she calls it Nineveh. Any reader of the biblical story of Jonah will know her meaning.

AF: According to one critic, your stories most encompass your literary prowess. Are your stories still dear to your heart?

CO: I have never stopped writing stories, and hope to have another collection before long. "The Bloodline of the Alkanas" appeared in *Harper's* in 2012, and a new story, "A Hebrew Sybil," is soon to be published in *Granta*. Nevertheless, some years ago, at a celebration of the twentieth anniversary of the founding of the Rea Award for the Short Story, John Updike remarked that he had arrived as a writer at a more fortunate time: when the short story was still a significant factor in the culture. A young writer beginning today, he said, would not be able to make a living through short stories, as he had. But the subject — and the issues it raises — goes far beyond the unlikelihood of selling to fewer and fewer magazines willing to publish stories. Most journals nowadays seek out the topical and the immediate — hence the ephemeral. The idea of a widely read magazine defined by its devotion to belles-lettres is as laughable as it is obsolete; what's wanted is *the news*.

Like Updike's (though never so successfully, it goes without saying), my early stories were written in that same period of the ascendancy of the short story. The major magazines all published stories; today, only two do. (My memory goes farther back, to childhood, when even newspapers featured what were called "short shorts," one-page narratives.) Gradually, and in some cases abruptly, the venues for stories began to vanish (e.g., the *Atlantic*), and though the academic writing workshops continue to turn them out, the readership for stories is drying up. Or, to say it more radically, literary reading itself is drying up. Gossip, topicality, celebrity, sensationalism take its place in the magazines. And the stories that are being written tend away from ambition toward smallness, toward what were once called "epiphanies," a large term for tiny quotidian recognitions. Who can imagine any American story equivalent to the reach and depth of Tolstoy's "The Death of Ivan Ilyich," or Chekhov's "Ward Six," or Chaim Grade's "My Quarrel with Hersh Rasseyner" or Lampedusa's "Ligeia"? All of these, for Americans, must be read in translation. And all are expansive: *long* stories; some would categorize them as novellas. But the workshops typically eschew the deeper imagination, and in one memorable period were dedicated to replications of Raymond Carver: i.e., stories short, dry, and small.

Of the stories in my *Collected Stories*, a British publication, I can only say that my heart was after the long and the large, and sometimes even the metaphysical. My favorite of all of them was written long ago, after I had first come upon Lampedusa's "Ligeia," which I stumbled on under the awkward title "The Professor and the Mermaid." I had never read anything so mysteriously enthralling. It inspired me to paraphrase it in some way, to transform it through another lens, and from this came what I still regard as the most successful story in the collection: "The Pagan Rabbi." I recall how, writing in the middle of the night (a lifelong habit), I puzzled over how to depict the nature of a dryad's speech. A dryad is a tree spirit; a tree is botanical, like odorous weeds and flowers; and suddenly it came to me that the dryad's "voice" must be in the form of a fragrance to be apperceived by the olfactory nerve. Such joy when I hit on that!

AF: What critera in your mind ties together the heterogeneous subject matter and characters in your stories?

CO: Criteria? Only that they were *there* when I was in the process of writing them. As for the relation between subject matter and character: an idea produces a situation, and a situation produces a character. Some writers may begin with a character, which then leads to a situation; but for me it is usually a wider notion that narrows into a conflicted condition. For instance, I have been mulling a story about two elderly poets, childhood friends, whose minds have acutely diverged, yet are compelled to meet after a lifetime of estrangement. One has achieved some celebrity as a modernist; the other is in eclipse, charged with archaism. What will happen at this crucial meeting (in the presence of a much younger person) I won't know until I begin to find out through the act of writing. Will it be a comedy? Possibly; though tinged with sadness. I suspect, though, that so-called "archaism" will win. And will I ever actually *write* this story?

(Addendum: I did. And archaism lost.)

AF: How did the idea to retell the story of Henry James's The Ambassadors *in* Foreign Bodies *come about? And what was your real goal in reversing the meaning of the classic?*

CO: What I had in mind was James's celebrated "international theme," the contrast between Europe and America that he repeatedly drew in his novels and stories. For James, Europe was sophisticated high civilization, a time-honored and unparalleled heritage of art and beauty and knowledge, while America stood for the raw, the naïve, the gauche, the untried, the unschooled, the foolishly innocent. But after the bloody darkness of the Second World War, it seemed to me, and particularly in the wake of the stench of the Holocaust, this contrast no longer held: Europe's heritage of art and beauty and knowledge had become radically steeped in chaos and slaughter, and it was America that shone. It's for this reason that I set Foreign Bodies in 1952, soon after the war (though it's not an America without impurity, since this was the period of the McCarthy scares). And whatever one thinks of America today, including its history of chattel slavery, treatment of Native Americans, incarceration of Japanese-Americans, one truth remains: the Holocaust didn't happen here. Still, to complicate things, the character who excoriates Europe in favor of America is far, far from admirable! So my intent was to turn Henry James's theme upside down and inside out — though not simplistically.

AF: What is the first book that really influenced you? How old were you when you read it?

CO: Omitting childhood reading and its profound influences (the inspiring character of the writer Jo in Little Women, the eeriness of Alice in Wonderland, and masses of fairy tales above all), I believe my first moment of adult transcendence-through-reading came at age seventeen, when I discovered, in a science fiction [!] anthology my brother brought home from the public library, Henry James's "The Beast in the Jungle," a story long enough to be called a novella. I read it and thought: *This is my life.* The next year, when I was a freshman in college, E.M. Forster's *The Longest Journey* was assigned in an English class, a novel I returned to time and time again over many decades.

AF: You've written on the subject of Henry James in several essays, but what is it about Henry James's writing that has so affected you? Was it the "craft" of his art, the psychological depth of his art, or both? Or anything else you could describe?

CO: Yes, craft and psychological depth. But also comedy! James is often overlooked as a satirist, and his dialogue frequently dances with comic wit. Beyond this, he possesses a discerning penetration into, not to put too fine a point on it (as HJ would say!), *evil*. His ghost stories, in particular "The Turn of the Screw," are permeated with it, and his drawing rooms can be poisoned arenas of malevolence: vide Gilbert Osmond in *The Portrait of A Lady*, or Kate Croy and Merton Densher in *The Wings of the Dove*. One might dare to say that James, unlike our contemporary culture, believes in the reality of evil.

AF: Of all the female characters in your books, which one is closest to your heart? Which one resembles you the most?

CO: Ruth Puttermesser, the hapless protagonist of *The Puttermesser Papers*. Though I have nothing else in common with her (she has never married, she is a failed lawyer, she manufactures a golem, she is brutally murdered), she is a bookish creature and sees the world through a literary lens, as (I fear) I sometimes do.

AF: Will you ever publish the private diary you have kept since 1953?

CO: No.

AF: The Nobel ever go to another Jewish writer?

CO: Possibly, and possibly to the extraordinary Israeli novelist A.B. Yehoshua (though I may be delusional to suppose this. But not likely ever again to any American Jewish writer. To a European Jewish writer? Not unlikely, if (as we have already seen) the theme is Holocaust; entirely unlikely, if the theme has any positive affinities with Israel or Zionism.

AF: Are you happy to be studied in US college courses on the Holocaust along with Primo Levi and Elie Wiesel?

CO: I am always grateful to be read at all. But *The Shawl*, the little book in question, is a work of fiction, while Levi and Wiesel write as victims and witnesses. Their work has the power of document. I would be happier if some other novel of mine had attracted the interest of the academy, since I am not entitled to be regarded as a "Holocaust writer."

AF: Why did you keep "The Shawl" hidden for seven years? What did you think of Sidney Lumet's direction of your play?

CO: I kept it in a drawer because I felt it to be anomalous and not quite legitimate. Anomalous: it had come to me in a rush, as if "dictated," a mystical notion I have always been quick to question. Not quite legitimate: it's my belief that the documents have the greater power of truth-telling. After all, the Holocaust deniers have even accused Anne Frank's *Diary* of being a fabrication. And much of the fiction based on the Holocaust has led to misrepresentation, fakery, and kitsch.

AF: The play directed by Sidney Lumet, also called "The Shawl" (although out of town, prior to its New York production, it was titled "Blue Light"), was actually a sequel to, rather than an adaptation of, the book. Its theme was, in fact, Holocaust denial. Lumet's two stagings were admirable.

AF: In a recent interview Don deLillo remarked that as long as there will be film, the novel will not die because the two are interchangeable.

CO: Interchangeable?! I couldn't disagree more. Film is always literal; the image is *there* before your eyes, the voices are in your ears, the interiors are meticulously furnished, a scene with water and trees will show you real water and real trees. You need imagine nothing;

everything is given, it's all a grand unalterable As Is, it's all a thinginess. Whereas a novel is yours for the making. It's true that film technique has influenced the novel in certain stylistic ways; yet the novel is always, always free, and film is always, always limited to its one imposed eye, an eye that isn't yours.

JS: Is it true that the novel is in danger, as you say in The Din in the Head?

CO: I'm afraid that was one miscreant reviewer's mistaken reading. What I actually wrote was: "The novel has not withered; it holds on, held in the warmth of the hand. . . . Life — the inner life — is not in the production of story lines alone, or movies would suffice. The din in our heads, that relentless inward hum of fragility and hope and transcendence and dread — where, in an age of machines addressing crowds, and crowds mad for machines, can it be found? In the art of the novel, in the novel's plasticity and elasticity. And nowhere else."

JS: Should your foreign translators be Jewish, perhaps in order to fully comprehend your literature?

CO: Whether the various translators of my work are Jewish or not, I have no idea. And how would it matter if they were or weren't? When we read nineteenth-century Russian novels and encounter such cultural oddities as, say, Name Days, and all those jaw-breaking patronymics, we aren't deterred and somehow assimilate it all. The wonder of reading fiction is that we can enter scenes and perceptions that we could otherwise never penetrate.

As for whether foreign readers can be open to my mostly American settings and mostly Jewish characters. I assume that serious readers, like genuinely literary readers everywhere, know that one reads fiction sometimes for the pleasure of recognition of the familiar, but other times in order to live other lives and experiences different from one's own — only to discover, all unexpectedly, the pleasure of recognition of the familiar. And think how we can find ourselves and our neighbors in Isaac Bashevi Singer's shtetl tales! If "universal" is to have any real meaning at all, it will be found in stories. And here we are in debt to translators, those magicians of language who allow us to understand and feel for people and societies unknown to us. Translation's blessing is that it unites, it does not divide.

ROOTS OF PASSION: ESSAYS ON *Cynthia Ozick*

JS: Please cite the most important influences in your writing career; please give a full list of writers, dead or alive. Which newer, contemporary writers seem promising?

CO: Of the classics, a fairly common and unsurprising list. E.M. Forster (especially *A Passage to India*); Henry James; Thomas Mann; George Eliot; Conrad (especially "The Secret Sharer"); Chekhov; Tolstoy (especially "The Death of Ivan Ilyich"); Lampedusa (*The Leopard*); Saul Bellow. I believe John Updike is likely to last, both for his language and for his chronicling of certain aspects of mid-century American society; and I have belatedly begun to read A.S. Byatt, and think her extraordinary, heads above her contemporaries. For the most part, though, I tend to reread rather than become acquainted with newer writing.

JS: Which of your contemporaries has been closest to writing the great American novel?

CO: If being alive at the same time counts as being a "contemporary," and if you will accept "a" rather than "the," then Saul Bellow has already written a great American novel, twice, with *The Adventures of Augie March* and *Herzog*. Mailer, who loudly lusted after the "the," failed even to achieve an "a." And after all, there can be only one "the," which some assign to *Huckleberry Finn*, and some to *The Great Gatsby*. If either of these deserves the solitary "the," it seems the contest has already been declared closed.

JS: You are considered to be a Jewish writer. Others may regard this as a superficial view, citing you and Philip Roth as being in the great canon of Historical Romance, one of the two great genres of American literature along with Realism, in which your so-called "Jewish" configurations are actually tropes, non-realistic, allegorical, typological figures like Hester Prynne, Moby Dick, or Billy Budd. Or let's say that your work and Roth's are as Hebraic as the New England Puritans' in that they are jeremiads —American jeremiads, as Sacvan Bercovitch states — as ritual designed to join social criticism to spiritual renewal, and public to private identity. What do you think of this?

CO: I think: Whew! What a majestic context! Philip Roth's monumentally acclaimed oeuvre has now been certified as an American classic, included as it is in the definitive Library of America series. And Hester Prynne, Moby Dick, and Billy Budd, even as they are uniquely individuated, are indeed "allegorical, typological" figures. I am grateful for the visionary quality this question implies, and am as moved and flattered by it as I am astonished — but I am wholly aware that my work can claim no place in so sublime a literary universe. And then there is this more immediate perplexity: in the painful act of writing, one can't think in such grand critical terms; one can only wrestle with the recalcitrance of words, syllable by syllable, phrase by phrase, sentence by stubbornly resisting sentence.

As for the term "Jewish writer," it is often shunned, most frequently, and in discomfort, by the writers to whom it is applied, because of the stigma it carries of the "parochial." Yet odd it is that no one bristles when William Styron is called a "Southern" writer, and Sarah Orne Jewett a "regional" writer, though each of these descriptions equals "parochial" defined as "narrow in scope." Yet who is more narrow in scope than Don Quixote, hailed as the most universal of character types?

olHolo

> *In a review of Bernard Malamud's collected work on the occasion of his joining the Library of America pantheon, I noted that the charge of parochial, from which he too recoiled (along with Bellow and Roth), was "never directed (and why not?) against Willa Cather's prairie Bohemians, or the denizens of Updike's Brewer or Faulkner's Yoknapatawpha" —a question that remains acutely relevant. And I ended the review with this query: "With all these believable Jews in hand, is Malamud a 'parochial' writer, after all? Yes, blessedly so, as every sovereign imaginative writer is obliged to be, from Dickens to Nabokov to Flannery O'Connor to Malamud himself: each one the sole heir to a singular kingdom."*
>
> *And finally, could you describe some aspects of your relationship with Dan Walden?*

Ode or haiku? Ode would require half an autobiography! Hence haiku, though in many more than seventeen syllables:

> Dan was my friend
> and friend of my family
> (daughter and son-in-law

and new baby, said baby
now about to start college),
but decades before,
Dan and Bea and I
were friends, having met
at MLA, laughing all the way,
and Bea and I ancestrally
were *landslayt*, she
from Horoduk,
located *hintn* Hlusk,
my own ancestral town.
We chimed, we rhymed,
we mimed our histories,
and in the Now of our lives
lived in letters
(first envelopes then email)
and literature,
and love.

Sections of Alessandra Farkas' questions and Cynthia Ozick's answers were extrapolated from Farkas' piece on Ozick in the Italian newspaper, *Corriere della Sera.*

8. Cynthia Ozick: A Jewish Woman Writer And Her Many Paradoxes [1]

Daniela Fargione

Cynthia Ozick is one of the most valued contemporary American writers, whose fiction, according to many critics, exemplifies "the Jewish writer oxymoron" (Ozick 1983: 178). Ozick respects the Jewish Covenant and its tradition, but she uses her imagination to invent stories; she worries about the temptations of paganism and the dangers of idolatry, but she fabricates fictional golems; she strongly refuses the label "woman writer", but she writes essays in defense of feminism, demanding equal rights with respect to the Torah; she despises the treatment of Jewish history (and of the Shoah in particular) as fiction, but she "cannot *not* write about it". In short, Cynthia Ozick's art resists narrow categorization and her fiction overcomes rigid confines, both literary and ideological. Dazzling and witty, erudite and irreverent, pugnacious and unpredictable, Cynthia Ozick's production includes hundreds of publications that embrace many different topics and genres: from short stories to literary reviews, from novels to translations, from poems to essays and drama. The aim of this study is to offer an analysis of Cynthia Ozick's literary work as representative of both contemporary American literature and Jewish culture.

---

[1] An earlier version of this article appeared in *Studi e ricerche. Quaderni del Dipartimento di Scienze del linguaggio e letterature moderne e comparate dell'Unversità di Torino*. Alessandria: Edizioni Dell'Orso, Vol. 3, 2008, pp. 149-169. ISBN: 978-88-62-7406-92. I wish to thank Edizioni dell'Orso for their kind permission to reprint it in this volume.

ROOTS OF PASSION: ESSAYS ON *Cynthia Ozick*

Cynthia Ozick and Jewish Literature

Both Ozick's literary work and criticism about her have recently largely expanded. Her first publications, however, received lukewarm responses, while her later novels and essays have been mostly considered as the quintessence of the "Jewish Idea" written by a devoted champion of Judaism. Steeped in the Jewish tradition with all its clashing viewpoints, Ozick's production has been misread for a long time, but the common tendency of critics to view Ozick's fiction solely as "a product of American Jewish writing [...] not only restricts Ozick's art severely, but it also erects rigid criteria by which art is to be judged" (Kauvar 1993a: xvii). Critical parochialism only denies her stubborn autonomy and her original unpredictability. Yet, despite Ozick's refusal of ethnic designation and cultural marginality, her fiction has often been seen as representing Jewish literary tradition only. This judgment may also justify her crucial position in a literary phenomenon that Lillian Kremer defines as "Jewish American literary renaissance" (Kremer 1993: 572).

Many current studies on Jewish American culture and literature have acknowledged "a renewal of interest, on the part of American Jews, in things Jewish" (Kauvar 1993b: 337). These last twenty years or so have witnessed an enormous and steady increase in the number of Jewish publications, a more tangible attention to both Judaic texts and *midrashic* narrative modes, a proliferation of scholarship on the Shoah and the State of Israel, and an expansion of Jewish literature courses and Jewish studies programs in both American and European universities. This unprecedented popularity has triggered a lively debate that has involved both the American reading public at large and the more specific circles of Jewish scholars in academia.

In the late 1960s and early 1970s many critics were predicting an approaching "Kaddish time" for Jewish writing[2], mainly due to the

---

2   Dershowitz, in *The Vanishing American Jew*, speaks of a possible "Kaddish time" (Kaddish is the prayer for the dead) for American Jewish Community. "But reports of the death of Judaism," he continues, "may be premature–if we can change the way we think and act about Jewish survival." According to Dershowitz "American Jewish life is in danger of disappearing, just as most American Jews have achieved everything we ever wanted: acceptance, influence, affluence, equality." This is mainly due to a "skyrocketing rates of intermarriage and assimilation, as well as 'the lowest birth rate of any religious or ethnic community in the United States.'" (Dershowitz 1998: 1, 6).

waning of the immigrant experience and the perils of assimilation (or "Yankeezation" to use one of Ozick's expressions). Eventually, prophecies of death have been dismissed. Far from being moribund, Jewish fiction has given proof of being vigorous, energetic, vibrant and, especially, diverse. However, one of the most important issues concerning Jewish literature that seems to function as a sort of common denominator among writers consists in the very definition of the subject in question. This is an eternal dilemma, the definition of "the indefinable" (Wirth-Nesher 1994: 3-12).

Many scholars have tried to locate different factors, which could determine the matrix of Jewish literature. A wide range of possibilities may be taken into account: from biological determinism (Jewish literature is literature written by Jews) to the specific themes explored (universal topics such as conflict between generations and ethical commitment), from religiosity (which implies some measure of suffering that ennobles human victims) to the domination of the written word or the written text (and thus the honor of being an intellectual), from the use of a specific language (Hebrew? Yiddish? Ladino? The author's language?) to a sacred respect for history (to which the issues of memory and heritage are attached). The fact remains that even though readers cannot approach any text completely ignoring a whole framework of expectations dictated by familiar myths and crystallized ideas about who is a Jew and what is Jewish literature, it is also true that more than one of these definitions may apply simultaneously. Hence, one single short story or novel may fit into more than one of the following categories: American fiction, Jewish fiction, Jewish-American fiction, Holocaust literature, Survivor testimony, and so on. Jewish literature, in this sense, seems to be destined to remain the product of a hyphenated culture.

Moreover, the difficulty of pinning down a satisfactory formula for identifying Jewish literature also arises from a general lack of familiarity with Jewish culture and tradition and –even more deplorable – a complete ignorance among American Jews of the classical texts that constitute the real skeleton of that very culture. This is the reason why Ozick constantly advocates a return to classical texts and to a particularism that would otherwise vanish.

Deeply concerned with the "precariousness of Jewish survival," as she explains in her article "All the World Wants the Jews Dead" (1974), Cynthia Ozick envisions Jewish life in modern America as weak, shallow, and punctuated by many empty rituals where food has substituted for liturgy by taking on an unholy meaning of collective redemption. In "Full Stomachs and Empty Rites" (1967) she sardonically lists the three necessary steps that a person has to accomplish in order to become a Jew: first s/he needs to visit a rabbi to learn about Ruth and Naomi; second, s/he needs to buy a star of David to wear on a gold chain around her/his neck; finally, s/he needs to learn how to cook *blintzes* (34). She concludes by claiming that the essence of American Jewish consciousness is "a pastrami sandwich; and all the rest is *Commentary*" (36). Jewish loyalty seems to find its last bastion in gastronomical celebrations at official religious offices. Against this trivialization of Jewish life, this collective forgetfulness of principles of faith and religious substance stands Cynthia Ozick's bold assumption that a Jew is "something more than *what* is. Being a Jew is something more than being an alienated marginal sensibility with kinky hair. Simply: to be a Jew is to be covenanted" (Ozick 1983: 122). Ozick reminds her readers that Jewish life is regulated by laws, by a series of precepts of Jewish conduct that, on the one hand reinforce Abraham's *brith* (covenant with God) and respect for tradition, on the other guarantee continuity and the transmittal of the original monotheistic values.

The paradox of being a "Jewish writer": Cynthia Ozick and idolatry
On more than one occasion it has been stated that the Jews are "the People of the Book." It is largely understood that Jewish people cherish a profound respect for and a strong bond with the written text, a preoccupation for the written word that comes from the very origins of the contract between God and His Chosen People. The survival of American Jewry, thus, seems to be dependent upon a return to text-centeredness as a resource for formulation, analysis, and understanding of the world because literature, Ozick claims, has to judge and interpret the world: "Story should not only be but mean" (Ozick 1989: 224).

One of the issues that the reader needs to understand in order to appreciate Cynthia Ozick's art is her definition of the Jewish writer and his/her function within a social context. In all her writings Cynthia Ozick displays an abiding sense of the past which encompasses tradition, memory, and heritage. History and devotion to the written word are the first tenets of her literary credo. However, this position strongly clashes with the lure and seductions of the assimilation process, which implies forgetfulness, so that Jews are doomed to remain in a marginal position, prey of alienation and parochialism, unless they escape "the descent into 'ethnicity'" (Ozick 1989: 224). She informs her readers that "to be a Jew is to be old in history [...] to be a member of a distinct civilization expressed through an oceanic culture in possession of a group of essential concepts and a multitude of texts and attitudes elucidating those concepts" (224). But anything written in the Diaspora, she warns, in order to survive "has to drive toward the matrix of the Jewish Idea" or to draw on liturgy, Torah, and Talmud. The investigation of the essence of Jewishness and the investigation of the essence of Jewish writing seem to be inextricable. Yet, to respond to the many critics and intellectuals who wanted to pin her down as the quintessence of "the Jewish Idea" and the spokesperson for an entire culture, Cynthia Ozick has responded at various times that,

> To be Jewish is to be a member of a civilization – a civilization with a long, long history, a history that is, in one way of viewing it, a procession of ideas. Jewish history is intellectual history. And all this can become the content of a writer's mind; but it isn't equal to a writer's mind. To be a writer is one thing; to be a Jew is another thing. To combine them is third thing. (Teicholz 1987: 172)

In *Art & Ardor* she also claims, "To me [...] the phrase Jewish writer [...] may be what rhetoricians call an 'oxymoron' – a pointed contradiction in which one arm of the phrase clashes profoundly with the other as to annihilate it" (Ozick 1983: 178). A Jewish writer, then, seems to be challenged by continuous bifurcations: the two worlds of art and Judaism cannot cohabit, as respect for the Word means avoidance of idolatry. The Second Commandment, in fact, is probably the most important precept of Judaic ethics and Cynthia Ozick's position toward idolatry is very well expressed in her 1979 essay "Literature as Idol: Harold Bloom". In this seminal essay she posits that the best way to describe a Jew is in negative terms: "A Jew is someone who shuns idols" (Ozick 1983: 188). An idol, she claims, "is obviously not only a little wooden graven image standing in the mud. Nor is an idol merely a false idea" (188), while in "The Riddle of the Ordinary," she explains that an idol is anything that intervenes between human beings and God, anything, in short, that is *"instead of* God" (207). Art and imagination and the sovereign precept of the Second Commandment collide – an artist is nothing other than a pagan idolater, and the two poles of this binary opposition are irreconcilable. Most of her short stories written in the 1970s are notable for the depiction of this crucial conflict. In the "Preface" to *Bloodshed* (a pivotal piece for understanding her literary aesthetics), she asserts that "the worry is this: whether Jews ought to be storytellers [...] Does the Commandment against idols warn us even against the ink?" (Ozick 1976: 10), but she also admits that the temptation is strong and that "to observe it is improbable, perhaps impossible" (Ozick 1983: 198).

It was only in the 1980s that Cynthia Ozick reconsidered her position: the relationship between imagination and idolatry was subject to "a major shift" as she admitted in an interview published in the *Paris Review* in 1987. In her conversation with Tim Teicholz she declares that she is "in the storytelling business" (168), but that she does not feel to be making idols any more as she does "no longer think of imagination as a thing to be dreaded" (167). This is primarily due to her urgency to meet the imperatives of ethical monotheism, which require "the largest, deepest, widest imaginative faculty of all [...] you simply cannot be a Jew if you repudiate the imagination" (168). Her condition of being *in-between* fosters compromise and leads her to distinguish between a "lower imagination, the weaker," which "falls to the proliferation of images," and a "strong imagination" that "can rise to the idea of the non-corporeal God" (167). Her thesis, in short, bestows on imagination the right to envision God, but while supporting this hypothesis her mind is conflicted: while art and Judaism continue to be "asymptotes" (Kauvar 1993c: 358), her prolific production witnesses a deliberate breach of Judaic orthodoxy.

The paradox of being a "Woman writer": Cynthia Ozick and feminism
The attempt to eschew any ideological constraints imposed by narrow designations is more vehemently expressed by Cynthia Ozick when the category at stake is that of the "woman writer". On May 15, 1997, she stated in an interview:

> I absolutely reject the phrase "woman writer" as anti-feminist. I wrote an essay about this as far back as 1977, at the height of the neo-feminist movement. It was becoming apparent then that there were going to be two categories of writers – writers and women writers – and, in fact, this has nearly come about. People often ask how I can reject the

phrase "woman writer" and not reject the phrase "Jewish writer" – a preposterous question. "Jewish" is a category of civilization, culture, and intellect, and "woman" is a category of anatomy and physiology. It's rough thinking to confuse vast cultural and intellectual movements with the capacity to bear children. (Katie Bolick, www.theatlantic.com)

One of the elements that strike the reader, here, is her admission of being a "Jewish writer". This phrase, it seems, has become less problematic than it was for her in the past. One wonders whether in recent years Cynthia Ozick has narrowed the distance between her two credos – belief in Judaism and belief in literature – or, on the contrary, whether in her mind the issue of women's condition (both social and artistic) has simply become more prevalent and/or urgent than the issue of being labeled "Jewish." Without doubt, Jewish women writers feel that their status still requires further debate and radical political change in order to attain acceptable recognition, and Cynthia Ozick's contribution has been crucial over the years to launching new challenging queries.

The essay she mentions in this conversation is "Literature and the Politics of Sex: A Dissent" (1977). This is one of two essays in the same collection (the other being "Previsions of the Demise of the Dancing Dog", 1971) that Ozick pairs under the significant title of "Justice to Feminism". The two pieces, she claims in an introductory note, are "'out of date'" because of the social and historical contexts they stem from, but they both share the same concern about women's exclusion (or self-exclusion) from a moment in history when the word "feminism" had not been uttered yet in the Jewish world. Even the language adopted, Ozick continues, is quite inappropriate, "the eerie gravity of the tone derives not so much from a pretense of authority as from the stiffness of the unused and the unfamiliar: a walk in new shoe-leather" (Ozick 1983: 261-62). Her walk is indeed quite a predicament, as the territory she penetrates is virginal and male hostility is harsh. In her first essay, the writer's polemic is directed toward "the ovarian/testicular theory of literature", a theory she discovered when she accepted a job as an instructor of English at a college of engineering. In her essay Ozick recalls that she was the only woman teacher in the department, but also that she began that illuminating experience without ever doubting that "the human mind was a democratic whole, androgynous, epicene, asexual" (264).

She eventually found out through different encounters that the most common myths about women and women writers have to do with the laws of physiology. She strongly criticizes the general tendency among male writers to equate the strivings of the artistic process with the "creativity' of childbearing", and she adds,

> To call a child a poem may be a pretty metaphor, but it is a slur on the labor of art. Literature cannot be equated with physiology, and woman through her reproductive system alone is no more a creative artist than was Joyce by virtue of his kidneys alone, or James by virtue of his teeth (which, by the way, were troublesome). (271)

One remarkable factor that stands out in her writing about the condition of women as artists and the myths concerning female identity is certainly her strong sense of humor. Sarah Blacher Cohen, who devoted a whole study to the "comic art" of Cynthia Ozick, deals with her "fumerism" (Cohen 1994: 148-78). This is the fusion of feminism and humor that Ozick fumes at the unjust approach to women's roles as artists. Her irony, however, is very biting and goes hand in hand with her brazen outspokenness.

With her essay "Literature and the Politics of Sex: A Dissent", Ozick resumes her old battle by subsuming male *and* female targets alike. These are the years when a New Left wing of postfeminists were proposing a *difference* between "'male' and 'female' states of intellect and feeling, hence of prose" (284). The writer strongly rebukes the ideology of separation and segregation in vogue at the time, by committing herself to a literature that "does not separate writers by sex, but that – on the contrary – engenders sympathies from sex to sex, from condition to condition […] Literature universalizes […] it does not divide" (285). Being a devotee of a "classical feminism," she cannot espouse the cause of this new kind of feminism and she concludes that "once you are allowed to get to your desk, a writer is a writer" (Kauvar 1985: 384). However, Ozick denounces the fact that if you are a woman you have "impediments that arise before you can get to your desk" (384). "In life" she recalls, "I am not free. In life, female or male, no one is free. In life, female or male, I have tasks; I have obligations and responsibilities" (Ozick 1983: 285).

The "illicitness" of the condition of the woman writer becomes a sort of a paradox if she is also Jewish. The complication arises from the fact that, as for Jewish writing, in general Jewish women writers can be situated within more than one world. Not only do they need to compete with a predominantly male literary establishment, but they also need to compete as representatives of a minority tradition. Their marginality is thus double: they are excluded from a secular gentile world, but they are also outsiders within their own tradition, as the world of words has always been the prerogative of Jewish men.

Yet, surprisingly, Ozick confirms her dual loyalty and controversial stance even with this issue. In her 1993 interview with Elaine Kauvar, she asserts that Judaism and feminism cannot be considered "in ultimate conflict" (372), as the Scripture is the first source of feminism. When we read that human beings were made in the image of the creator, we also have "the primary text making feminist statements – that is, if feminism is to be defined as holding the sexes as equal in worth" (372). She concludes by saying that although she does not defend the "patriarchal hypotheses" that indeed she recognizes, she also claims that "the sociology of Jewish women, their living reality, has contradicted many of these patriarchal assumptions" (372).

Eventually, women writers began to search a personal, vibrant, and energetic style to give voice to their innermost thoughts and feelings. Cynthia Ozick has certainly found her own and yet, Ozick explains, the achievement of bliss originated by responding to her innate artistic drive is a gradual process. It is, more specifically, a gradual demise. The writer must first get rid of the many "responsibilities" and "obligations" that both religious strictures and practical life impose on her. "In life I am not free," Cynthia Ozick writes, but she also states:

> When I write I am free. I am, as a writer, whatever I wish to become. I can think myself into a male, or a female, or a stone, or a raindrop, or a block of wood, or a Tibetan, or the spine of a cactus... When I write, I am in command of a grand *As If*. I write *As If* I were truly free. And this *As If* is not a myth. As soon as I proclaim it, as soon as my conduct as a writer expresses it, it comes into being. (Ozick 1989: 285-286)

ROOTS OF PASSION: ESSAYS ON *Cynthia Ozick*

The act of writing entails the complete freedom of the writer. However, the artistic creation is a corridor that leads the way to both freedom and idolatry.

Cynthia Ozick and biography

If Ozick's major concern is to come to terms with the conflict of art and idolatry, the relationship between an artist's life and artistic production is of great significance. In her collection of essays, *Quarrel & Quandary* (2000), Ozick states that "Biography, or call it life, attaches to certain writers – but only to certain writers – with the phantom tenacity of a Doppelgänger: history clouding into fable" (127). The kinship of fiction and biography is evident in much of her literary work and both serve the same purpose: to judge the world. The reconstruction of lives in her fiction, as much as the biographical profiles of real people in her essays (mainly writers or philosophers), have the same aim: "to evoke believability in a story about the perilous span between birth and death" (Ozick 1989: 133). One an artificial fabrication and the other a product of memory, fiction and biography are so intertwined that Ozick wonders which of the two "is the apprentice, which the master?" "If it is true" she continues, "that the novel in its infancy set out to imitate life, then one might say that biography's narrative-of-fact is the first form, the Ur-Gestalt, the predecessor-pattern […] But if biography is the art of organizing a coherent tale out of the chancy scatterings and sunderings of any individual life, then surely biography would seem to be the imitator, and the novel is the model" (132). And yet, she concludes, it is biography with its "honest constancy of its narrative ripeness" that still *inspires* us. Inspiration, however, does not stem from the multitude of events that make up individual lives; rather, from the inherited ancestry attached to personal histories. Ozick's process in the recreation of somebody's life can be compared to a historical retrieval. She is not interested in single facts because they only provide partial insights. What she aims at is the reconstruction of people's legacies.

A typical example of this technique is provided by her collection of short stories about her alter ego, Ruth Puttermesser. The first of her Puttermesser's stories appeared in 1977 in *The New Yorker* with the title "Puttermesser: Her Work History, Her Ancestry, Her Afterlife." When we meet the eponymous heroine for the first time, Puttermesser lives in New York City. She is thirty-four, a lawyer, also "something of a feminist, not crazy" (Ozick 1997: 3), certainly not attractive, but neither "bad-looking," despite the fact that she has "one of those Jewish faces with a vaguely Oriental cast" (5). Molded after Ozick herself and her lawyer husband, Puttermesser is depicted in the first story as a sort of polymath. An overachiever at school, she now studies Hebrew grammar in bed, fascinated as she is by the mysterious, "stunning mechanism" of the language. She indulges in her "weakness for fudge," though she "immediately afterward furiously brushed her teeth, scrubbing off guilt" (13): Puttermesser is, after all, a true "compulsive-compulsive." She is intellectually engaged; she plays herself at chess and pins up all the *New York Times* crosswords she can find. She works for a "blueblood Wall Street firm," where "though a Jew and a woman, she felt little discrimination"(6). After three years, however, she gets fired and accepts an offer at the Department of Receipts and Disbursements, where "most were Italians and Jews" (10). While working in the shabby Municipal Building, Puttermesser's fancy rises up to the point to go beyond the hideous greyness and trivialities of her everyday life. She nurtures "a luxuriant dream, a dream of *gan eydn*," a Garden of Eden, which is to say "the World to come" (12). She imagines it as her afterlife but here Ozick comments: "to postulate an afterlife was her single irony – a game in the head not unlike a melting fudge cube held against the upper palate" (13). The insatiable passions of Puttermesser, eating fudge and reading books forever, finally find a licit territory where they can be satisfied: her imagination. The sweetness of chocolate fudge juxtaposes with her bookish pleasures, but this vision of her "afterlife" is tightly connected to the reconstruction of her "ancestry": her journey toward the future must be preceded by a journey *à rebours*. To achieve command of the Hebrew language is her first step toward the reconstruction of her family tree. She states that "Twice a week, at night (it seemed), she went to Uncle Zindel for a lesson" (14). But it only seemed so… The old man, a former *shammes* (a synagogue sexton), a surrogate father, is the symbol of her family heritage and past; he is the memory, the one who, together with the intricacies and mystical fascination of the Hebrew language, can possibly quench her thirst for information. An extravagant scene is reported in the book, but only to be abruptly interrupted by the narrator:

> Stop. Stop, stop! Puttermesser's biographer, stop! Disengage, please. Though it is true that biographies are invented, not

recorded, here you invent too much. A symbol is allowed, not an entire scene: do not accommodate too obsequiously Puttermesser's romance. Having not much imagination, she is literal with what she has. (16)

Readers understand that their heroine's biography is quite slippery, as Uncle Zindel had died four years before the recollection of this episode, which, obviously, never occurred if not in Puttermesser's mind. Ozick instills the doubt on the very notion of "Jewish identity," one of the central themes of this destabilized narrative pastiche, and pinpoints the necessity to ward off the dangers of Jewish extinction, as well as of the perils of artistic fantasy. The artistic creation, if given excessive freedom, may become idolatrous.

"Puttermesser is not to be examined as an artifact," the author writes in the opening pages, "but as an essence. Who made her? No one cares…" but she concludes, "Hey! Puttermesser's biographer! What will you do with her now?" (19). Simply, she will continue narrating her story, and her readers, after witnessing a process of redemption of her past and catching a glimpse of her ideal future, can finally and unexpectedly see their heroine plunged in Paradise. "Puttermesser in Paradise" concludes this series of stories, but before depicting her in Eden, she is described in her last scene, before her death. Ozick's novel comes to an end as Puttermesser's life comes to an end. "A good biography," Ozick explains in an essay, "is itself a kind of novel. Like the classical novel, a biography believes in the notion of 'a life' – a life as a triumphal or tragic story with a shape, a story that begins at birth, moves on to the middle part, and ends with the death of the protagonist" (Ozick 1983: 6).

Puttermesser ascends to heaven, where all her desires are finally fulfilled. She marries a guy who turned her down when she was in college, and at last she gives birth to a baby boy. However, despite her happiness, the narrator tells us that "There is a flaw in Eden" (233), which is no serpent, no expulsion, nor angels with their flaming swords. All that belongs to children's fairy tales. In paradise, she concludes, there is no time and "Timelessness does not promise the permanence of any experience. Where there is no time, there is no endurance. Without the measure of time, what is lastingness?" In paradise nothing is permanent, everything is ephemeral, and happiness soon transforms itself into preternatural unhappiness. Every "display of splendor" has its counterpart in decay;

every hint of success precludes a fall; any wonderful appearance, a fading away. After spending her entire life longing for Eden, now that she resides in it Puttermesser yearns for a coming back; at last, this innocuous butter knife (Puttermesser in Yiddish), has acquired the power to cut through life and understand its ultimate meaning. Puttermesser's biography concludes with her awareness that the Solomon's Truth is that "The secret meaning of Paradise is that it too is hell" (234).

Puttermesser's stories reveal how Cynthia Ozick assumes the self-conscious role of autobiographer. However, instead of investing herself with the authority of an omniscient narrator who provides a faithful chronicle, she instills doubts about her objectivity. While revealing the author's fallacies, she underscores her central preoccupation: the freedom of art and the perils of idolatry.

Cynthia Ozick and Language
Language, for Cynthia Ozick, is one of the main issues in the construction of Jewish identity and her attention to style partly depends on her respect for the written word. According to Susan Klingenstein, her fictions are written "in the intellectual grammar of rabbinic thought" (51), whose morphology is inscribed and prescribed in the very first verses of Genesis, which declare Judaism's fundamental tenet of separation of the divine and the material. This axiom implies that, although nature has been created by God, nature is not inhabited by Him, as Ozick so strongly expresses in many of her short stories, among which "The Pagan Rabbi" (1971) is the most exemplary. The major quandary that arises from the separation of these two incommensurable realms – the human and the divine – consists in finding an effective resolution which could bridge this chasm and allow humanity to establish some sort of relation with God. The formula that the Torah offers is that of the *brith*, the contractual association between God and humanity through Abraham's Covenant. Moreover, the Torah (which holds the position of the most important book of reference for Jewish history as it narrates how to inherit and pass on the legacy of the Covenant) also indicates that the identity of Jewish people arose in the desert, in nobody's land. However, by virtue of belonging to that very Promised Land, to an absence rather than to a presence, the Torah acquired a universal value, as it was proclaimed simultaneously in the "seventy languages" of the world. Ozick herself reminds us of the legend according to which "the Septuagint – the oldest

Greek version of the Hebrew Bible – came to be written: seventy sages, we are told, entered seventy separate chambers, and emerged with seventy copies of an identical text" (Ozick 1989: 199).

In this sense, Moses was the very first translator of God for his Chosen People, and his task of translating was not merely linguistic. In Deuteronomy 29: 29 Moses warns the people of Israel that "The secret things belong onto the Lord our God; but the things that are revealed belong unto us and to our children for ever, that we may *do* all the words of this law."³ The accent, as Klingenstein highlights, is on the verb "to do," because God's word needs to be translated into action. This is a central idea in Judaism, since the Sinaitic Commandment yokes the Jews to both history and exile. While their involvement in life is permanent, their location is instead temporary. What is intrinsic in the condition of the Chosen People is a perpetual dislocation that involves both the land where they reside and their language. The Jewish writer in English, or in any other language but Hebrew, "is exiled twice from the irrecoverability of an original language" (Wirth-Nesher 1994: 6).

Cynthia Ozick also feels to be a sort of *zwischenmensch*, a "between person" (Walden 1987: 1), facing the dilemma of being at the center of a conflict between tradition and the world at large. Ruth R. Wisse defines this tension as the situation of somebody "who is native to two cultures while fully at home in neither" (Bloom 1986: 36). As Kauvar remembers, the condition is captured in a consolidated formula: "a Jew at home is a man abroad" (1993b: 338). This sense of uneasiness of the Jewish author writing in the Diaspora is expressed by Ozick in her preface to *Bloodshed*. She claims that "A language, like a people, has a history of ideas […] English is a Christian language. When I write in English, I live in Christendom. But if my postulates are not Christian postulates, what then?" (Ozick 1976: 9).

Language is certainly a crucial issue for contemporary Jewish writers in prose, and with Cynthia Ozick the trap of being caught between two languages, between two cultures, enlarges the discussion of the meaning of language to a discussion of the meaning of history, inheritance, and tradition. When in 1970 she participated in the Eighth Annual American-Israel Dialogue in Jerusalem, she presented her programmatic essay "America: Toward Yavneh," later included in *Art & Ardor* with the title

---

3   For further discussion on this issue see Susan Klingestein 1997: 51 and following pages. My italics.

"Toward a New Yiddish." Irreverent as usual, she shocked her audience by articulating a thesis "in dispraise of Diaspora" (Ozick 1983: 156), which centered around "a revulsion against the values [...] of the surrounding culture itself: a revulsion against Greek and pagan modes, whether in their Christian or post-Christian vessels, or whether in their purely literary vessels, or whether in their vessels of *Kulturgeschichte*" (156). Discarding the Zionist tenet, according to which Israel should be the center of Jewry, she talks about her own marginality not as "a source of liberation, but rather a worrisome buzz in the back of the mind" (159). As the Diaspora can be considered as a "Jerusalem Displaced," she believes that "America shall, for a while, become Yavneh" (160). Ozick explains in a note that Yavneh was a small town, where an academy was established with Roman permission after the fall of Jerusalem and the destruction of the temple. It was in Yavneh that the Chosen People – a people in *galut* (exile) – identified learning as a substitute (or a surrogate) for homeland.

At this point of her lecture, Ozick said aloud what her audience was probably thinking silently: how can this be possible when all the Jewish people in America "speak a Gentile language and breathe a Gentile culture?" (174). The answer was quite unexpected, as she proclaimed that the solution could be found in the ambitious project of learning a new language that she called, in fact, "New Yiddish," a sort of Judaized English with a liturgical nature. Eventually, in 1983 when she published her essay "Bialik's Hint," she refused her earlier theory of the new language – "my old fantasy" (238) – and proposed a "new alternative," an "unimaginable fusion" of the "intellectual power" promoted by the Enlightenment with "Jewish sensibility" (239). This shift was mainly a result of the fact that Ozick's speculations about the power of language changed along with her position on writing as a Jew. "Language can brilliantly clarify," she admits, but "it can also create, just as brilliantly, the Big Lie [...] In fiction – which is a lie that tells the truth – it can do both" (Rainwater 1983: 263).

It is true that the commingling of the two cultures and languages, as Ozick foresaw, was an "inevitability." The process of Jewish cultural assimilation in the texture of American society triggered a mixing of vernacular American and Yiddish, from which a bastardized dialect, often called "Yinglish," sprang. This dialect still survives in its spoken form among the Jewish immigrants of the second generations. Contamination of the two languages was tantamount to a domestication of the Jewish vernacular on the one side, and to an absorption of Yiddish into American English on the other. But the consequent transformations of both languages could not happen in a vacuum, that is, independently from culture. The yearning for respectability that generally was at the origin of this phenomenon was particularly true for the *Amerikaner-geborene*, those born in the United States. All these issues are splendidly revealed in one of Ozick's most successful long stories: "Envy; or, Yiddish in America" (1969). Here, its seventy-six-year old protagonist, the Yiddish poet Hersheleh Edelshtein, is depicted as the custodian of some familiar themes: Jewish identity, idolatry, the condition of the artist.

    The story can be read in many different ways, since various layers of interpretation are applicable at different levels. On a first level the themes of the Jewish artist and his identity surface. While clinging to his Jewishness, Edelshtein also craves recognition from the surrounding gentile world; his major problem, which soon becomes a catch-22, does not depend on personal talent, but instead on the character's cultural rootlessness and sense of alienation. Edelshtein, in fact, does not belong to the generation of Jews who have grown in the American Diaspora, nor does he belong to the modern Manhattan gentile society either. A widower and childless, he is the author of four volumes of poems written in Yiddish by which he has earned some respectability among Yiddishists. However, because his verses have never been translated into English, he has never attained the high standard of excellence that he wishes for. Edelshtein, whose surname in English means "refined stone," is treated with caustic irony. His major concern is to find a translator who could free him from perpetual anonymity and save him from an "unmarked grave" (78), by transforming his "'refined stones'" into "poetic jewels" (Cohen 1994: 48).

    On a deeper level, "Envy" can be read as a parable grounded in Judaic teachings, since Ozick the prophet inveighs against the demise of Yiddish as the vessel of an entire culture. This is a phenomenon that she describes in terms that convey a pervasive sense of grief and death. Yiddish, in fact, is the language that perished dramatically in the Shoah and that strives to survive in America, although only in atrophied forms and among decrepit people. Edelshtein remembers that "the language was lost, murdered. The language – a museum. Of what other language can it be said that it died a sudden and definite death, in a given decade, on a given piece of soil?" (42). Edelshtein, a sort of entertaining stand-up comedian, reads and lectures in Yiddish in front of ignorant synagogue audiences who know nothing about their own origins and culture, and for whom Yiddish is no more than the vehicle for funny vulgar expressions. To this *Amerikaner-geboren* generation symbolized by Hannah (the young translator he courts, but who refuses to translate him because he is not interesting enough), he screams to "go get a memory operation" (97). Cultural amnesia corresponds to a renunciation of history.

Ultimately, the undiscussed protagonist of "Envy; or, Yiddish in America," is language itself. Cynthia Ozick allows Yiddish to penetrate the texture of its prose and to resound in many different ways. The opening paragraph can be seen as an effective example of a linguistic strategy in which, by using Yiddish words or phrases, she sets the main character's point of view and the ironic tone that she adopts to express this viewpoint. The Yiddish expression "*Amerikaner-geboren*" that Edelshtein uses as his deepest vituperation against the novelists of "Jewish extraction" is translated as "spawned in America" (Ozick 1995, 41). This idiomatic expression suggests the cultural background of Edelshtein's reflections and is also used to satirize his personal sense of inadequacy and frustration for not being able to attain a voice on his own in the American belletristic milieu.

Moreover, the text is heavily interspersed with words taken from the Yiddish lexicon. On the very first page, for example, idioms such as *mamaloshen*, *cheder-yinglach*, and *malamed*, and phrases such as *Juderrein is Kulturrein*,[4] are simply inserted in Ozick's English prose, as if *these* were shiny precious stones, mounted as jewels. This linguistic technique is very effective, as the reader is immediately set in a linguistically hybrid territory, which keeps the flavor of an ancient past. By making Yiddish a sort of mocking dialect, especially when the grammatical structure of English is interspersed with word inversions, omissions, or inadequate subordinations, Ozick creates a third idiom. This language allows her to convey all her contempt for that "generation" of Jewish American writers who still use a shadow of the Yiddish language to cling to a tradition to which they no longer belong. For these authors, Yiddish happens to be a pretext to flatter a certain portion of the American reading public and to attain literary fame by ethnic wit.

---

4   *Mamaloshen* means "mother tongue"; *cheder-yinglach* refers to a boy pupil of Jewish religious school; *malamed* is a preacher; *Judenrein is Kulturrein* means Judaism is culture.

Ozick emphasizes the relevance of language to build a discourse on Jewish identity and on the idiocy of the literary establishment that perpetuates archetypal stereotypes of the Jews. Examples come from the series of stilted letters that Edelshtein writes to Ostrover's editors. Edelshstein's pompous artificial style is an open attack on his hypocrisy, as he only pretends to bemoan the waning of Yiddish, while he actually weeps the lack of an appreciative audience for his verses, thus exposing all his *yetser harah*, his desire for fame.

Edelshtein firmly believes that the attainment of literary success can be sanctioned by translation, as the hegemony of the English language would also allow marginal texts to move to the center of a cultural discourse. The dying condition of Yiddish may be revitalized by a rescue effort of an English translator, a figure that acquires a crucial function in the story. Ostrover himself, a "cripple" (55) in English, owes his international fame to an army of translators that he changes frequently, using them as a stool: "He stands on the back of hacks to reach" (55), the spinster hack writes in a letter of reply to Edelshtein, informing him about her role as one of Ostrover's translators. The quality of the poet's Yiddish is disputable, she adds, but after all this is not so important, because what matters here is the magic "transformation" that *she* achieves: "It's all cosmetics, I'm a cosmetician, a painter, the one they pay to do the same job on the corpse in the mortuary, among them […] I tell you his Yiddish doesn't matter" (56). Here the translator's task is to touch up the aesthetic quality of Ostrover's prose and to manipulate the original text in such a manner as to respond to the expectations of the American reading public. The issues that Ozick probes are fidelity in translation and the invisible role of translators. The "spinster hack" is completely aware of being "used" by Ostrover; however, she admits that she gets "a little glory out of it" (54) and that her identity changes too, acquiring some sort of value: "[…] with Ostrover on my back I'm something else: I'm 'Ostrover's translator.' You think that's nothing? It's an entrance into *them*. I'm invited everywhere, I go to the same parties Ostrover goes to" (55).

As Lawrence Venuti (1995) has eloquently argued, "Invisibility" is the translator's common condition in the American context and it is also indirectly proportional to the fluency attained in the translated text. If a translated work reads fluently, it is considered transparent. "If a translation seems flawless," Cynthia Ozick states in her essay "A Translator's Monologue" ("we take it to be authoritative; if it is authoritative, we trust its importance; if we can trust its importance, we know it will be useful. And by 'useful' I mean that a translation can serve as a lens into the underground life of another culture" (199). But this thesis, she concludes, is "false" (198). According to Venuti, translation is required "to efface its second-order status," producing "the illusion of authorial presence whereby the translated text can be taken as the original" (Venuti 1995, 7). This process of domestication of the original is defined as "narcissistic," since fluent translations provide readers with "the experience of recognizing their own culture in a cultural other" (15). The process of domestication that Ostrover's translators attain with their linguistic manipulation challenges the notion of authorship, as they are producers of those literary texts as much as the original writer is. The translators, in fact, are involved in a creative process as much as the author of the original text. As Cohen's reading of the story highlights, both Ostrover and the spinster hack "possess comic affectation, for he thinks he is the only real Yiddish literary genius, and she 'fancied herself the *real* Ostrover'" (56). Cohen claims that Ozik's ironic treatment of Ostrover is visible in his ploys to gain fame through "hoaxes of translation." She adds that if "reading an author's work in translation is, as Bialik notes, 'kissing the bride through the veil,' then so many deft hands have improved the appearance of Ostrover's bride that she scarcely resembles his flawed original" (55). In a letter to Edelshtein, the spinster hack compares her relationship with Ostrover to "a marriage" (55). An intimate, secret bond is established between the author and his translator as between a bride and a groom. "Like a wife," the spinster hack continues, "I have the supposedly passive role. Supposedly: who knows what goes on in the bedroom?" (55). Here, the postulate of faithfulness to the original eventually proves to be false, as there is no original text or, better, there are too many.

The translators' intellectual efforts, however, do not result in their recognition; the author's fame shines on them too but only by reflection. Their work is never completely acknowledged publicly; they remain in a secondary position, while their intervention in the original, their rewriting of a rewritten foreign text, responds to a specific political agenda which reinforces domestic values. When these values happen to be Yankeefied Jewish values, the distortion is immense, and the perpetuation of crystallized stereotypes is guaranteed.

As we have seen, then, in the attempt to forge her literary identity Ozick tackles various modes to express her voice. A multiplicity of forms obviously implies a multiplicity of languages and styles. With no doubts, her many talents prove that she is an extraordinary living contradiction, an exuberant artist who, while living *in-between* a paradox, feels perfectly *at home* with herself and with any literary form.

WORKS CITED

Bloom, Harold (ed.). 1986. *Modern Critical Views: Cynthia Ozick*. New York: Chelsea House.

Bolik, Katie. "The Many Faces of Cynthia Ozick". 15 May 1997. *The Atlantic Online*.

http://www.theatlantic.com/past/docs/unbound/factfict/ozick.htm.

Cohen, Sarah Blacher. 1994. *Cynthia Ozick's Comic Art: From Levity to Liturgy*. Bloomington: Indiana University Press.

Dershowitz, Alan M. 1998. *The Vanishing American Jew. In Search of American Identity for the Next Century*. New York: Simon & Schuster.

Kauvar, Elaine M. 1985. "An Interview with Cynthia Ozick". *Contemporary Literature* 26 (4): 375-401.

—. 1993a. *Cynthia Ozick's Fiction. Tradition and Invention*. Bloomington and Indianapolis: Indiana University Press.

—. 1993b. "Introduction: Some Reflections on Contemporary American Jewish Culture." *Contemporary Literature* 34 (3): 337-357. Special issue: *Contemporary American Jewish Literature*.

—. 1993c. "An Interview with Cynthia Ozick." *Contemporary Literature* 34 (3): 358-94.

Kremer, Lillian S. 1993. "Post-Alienation: Recent Directions in Jewish-American Literature." *Contemporary Literature*, 34 (3): 571-591.

Klingestein, Suzanne. 1997. "'In Life I Am Not Free': The Writer Cynthia Ozick and Her Jewish Obligations". *Daughters of Valor: Contemporary Jewish American Women Writers*, ed. Jay L. Halio and Ben Siegel, 48-79. Newark: University of Delaware.

Ozick, Cynthia. 1966. "The Pagan Rabbi" *Hudson Review* (19): 425-54. Reprinted in *Explorations: An Annual on Jewish Themes*. Ed. Murray Mindlin and Chaim Bermont (1968); in *My Name Aloud: Jewish Stories by Jewish Writers*, ed. Harold U. Ribalow (1969); in *Best SF:1971*, ed. Harry Harrison and Brian W. Aldiss (1972); in *The Pagan Rabbi and Other Stories* (1971; Syracuse UP 1995); in *Jewish American Stories*, ed. Irving Howe (1977); in *The Penguin Book of Jewish Stories*, ed. Emanuel Litvinoff (1979); in *More Wandering Stars: An Anthology of JewishFantasy and Science Fiction*, ed. Jack Dann (1981).

—. 1967. "Full Stomachs and Empty Rites" *Congress By-Weekly*, 34: 34-35.

—. 1970. "America: Toward Yavneh." *Judaism* 19: 264-82. Reprinted in *Congress Bi-Weekly*, 26 February 1971; reprinted as "New Yiddish: Language for American Jews" in *Jewish Digest* 18 (1973); in *Art & Ardor* (1983).

—. 1974. "All the World Wants the Jews Dead." *Esquire* 82: 103-7.

—. 1975. "The Riddle of the Ordinary." *Moment* (1): 55-59. Reprinted in *Art & Ardor* (1983).

—. 1976. *Bloodshed and Three Novellas*. New York: Knopf (Dutton/Obelisk, 1983).

—. 1977. "Justice to Feminism: 2. Literature and the Politics of Sex: A Dissent." *Ms*. Reprinted in *Art & Ardor* (1983).

—. 1983. "Bialik's Hint." *Commentary* 75: 22-28. Reprinted in *Metaphor & Memory* (1989).

—. 1983. "Literature as Idol: Harold Bloom." In *Art & Ardor* (1983). Reprinted as "Of Polished Mirrors" in *The Writer in the Jewish Community: An Israeli-North American Dialogue*, eds. Richard Siegel and Tamar Sofer. Rutherford, N.J.: Fairleigh Dickinson University Press.

—. 1983. *Art & Ardor: Essays*. New York: Knopf. (Dutton/Obelisk, 1984).

—. 1989. *Metaphor & Memory: Essays*. New York: Knopf.

—. 1989. "A Translator's Monologue" in *Metaphor & Memory: Essays*. New York: Knopf. First published in *Prooftext* 3: 1-8, 1983.

—. 1995. "Envy; or, Yiddish in America" in *The Pagan Rabbi and Other Stories*. Syracuse: Syracuse University Press. First published in *Commentary* 48: 35-53. Reprinted in *The Best American Short Stories*, ed. M. Foley and D. Burnett (1970); in *The Pagan Rabbi and Other Stories* (1971); in *A Cynthia Ozick Reader*, ed. Elaine Kauvar (1996).

—. 1997. *The Puttermesser Papers*. New York: Knopf.

—. 2000. *Quarrel & Quandary*. New York: Knopf.

Rainwater, Catherine and William J. Scheick. 1983. "An Interview with Cynthia Ozick ". *Texas Studies in Literature and Language* 25: 255-65.

Teicholz, Tim. 1987. "The Art of Fiction XCV." *Paris Review* 102: 154-90.

http://www.theparisreview.org/interviews/2693/the-art-of-fiction-no-95-cynthia-ozick.

Venuti, Lawrence. 1995. *The Translator's Invisibility: A History of Translation*. London and New York: Routledge.

Walden, Daniel. 1987. "Introduction". In *The World of Cynthia Ozick*. Special issue of *Studies in American Jewish Literature,* ed. Daniel Walden. 6: 164-67.

Wirth-Nesher, Hana (ed. and introd.). 1994/5754. *What is Jewish Literature?* Philadelphia, Jerusalem: The Jewish Publication Society.

www.ingramcontent.com/pod-product-compliance
Lightning Source LLC
Chambersburg PA
CBHW070202100426
42743CB00013B/3018